The Content Management Handbook

The Content Management Handbook

Martin White

facet publishing

© Martin White 2005

Published by
Facet Publishing
7 Ridgmount Street
London WC1E 7AE

Facet Publishing is wholly owned by CILIP: the Chartered Institute of Library and
Information Professionals.

First published 2005

British Library Cataloguing in Publication Data
A catalogue record for this book is available from the British Library.

ISBN 1-85604-533-1

Typeset in 11/14 pt New Baskerville and MicroSquare by Facet Publishing.
Printed and made in Great Britain by MPG Books Ltd, Bodmin, Cornwall.

To
Cynthia, Nick and Simon

Contents

Preface

FOR MUCH OF the last decade the information profession has been trying to establish a role in knowledge management. In the late 1990s there was much talk about the need for organizations to have Chief Knowledge Officers, and this seemed to offer excellent career prospects. Things have not quite worked out that way. Now the pendulum has swung in the other direction, and instead of looking downstream at knowledge management opportunities information professionals are starting to look at the up-stream opportunities presented by content management.

However, content management is almost as hard to describe and envision as knowledge management, and the borders between content management, document management and records management (to say nothing of digital asset management and other related technologies) are blurred. That is not going to change because technology, especially the use of XML, fails to see any difference between a content object that might be a map on a website and another that might be a table in a report on an intranet.

The opportunities for the information profession in supporting the development of effective content management systems in organizations that can then be implemented using content management software (CMS) products are immense. My own estimate is that there are probably around 300,000 intranets in the UK. Even if this is wrong by a factor of ten that still leaves some 30,000 intranets, most of which are probably the information equivalent of a black hole. Information is poured in, but nothing escapes.

Without a content management strategy (CMS) there cannot be a content management system (CMS) and without a content management system (CMS) there is no point in implementing content management software. This is especially the case if the organization has a client/contact management system (CMS) or a case management system (CMS). The potential for confusion with this particular three-letter acronym is considerable. I have taken the view that since you cannot have a CMS without a CMS without a CMS I will use the acronym in a fairly cavalier way. That may not appeal to the purists, but I make no apology.

Information professionals have a very significant opportunity to shape the content management strategy of their organizations, carrying out information audits and looking at how internal and external information can best be integrated. Any such strategy has to have a user-centric approach, and this opens up the chance to use new techniques, notably persona development and scenarios, to understand not only how people find information but also what they do with it. Workflow analysis and the development of metadata schemes, and looking in detail at approaches to search and findability are also involved, and behind all of this is the increasing awareness of the principles and practice of information architecture.

The end result is that there is virtually no area of any of the three CMS definitions where information professionals cannot make a significant and on-going contribution to the effective management of content, and thus information and knowledge, in any organization that is struggling to cope with business in the 21st century.

There are already some excellent books on content management, notably the *Content Management Bible* by Bob Boiko (2002) and *Managing Enterprise Content* by Ann Rockley et al. (2002). This book hopefully complements these by taking a project view of what it takes to get from wondering how implementing a CMS could benefit the organization through specifying, selecting and procuring a CMS product, to implementing the product on time and on budget.

My aim with this book is to try to highlight both the benefits of CMS and the risks in ill-considered deployments. In an intranet project the CMS will have an impact on every desktop, the only software application other than word processing and e-mail that will have an impact on every employee. And every visitor to a poorly executed website will need a lot of persuading to return.

The book is written from my own personal experience, and is the way that I work with my clients on CMS projects. Hopefully the mistakes I have made and then learnt from will be of benefit to you. Around the world there is a group of CMS consultants all trying to find better ways of advising their clients, and now there is a CM Professionals organization (www.cmprofessionals.org) that has been started in the USA to provide support to both the consulting profession and content managers working within organizations. Good practice is still evolving and will do for many years to come. I have no doubt that if I am asked to write a second edition it will be quite different, if only because the cost of CMS products is decreasing rapidly and the ease of implementation is increasing, albeit not quite so rapidly!

I would like to thank Tony Byrne, Bob Boiko, Bob Doyle, Howard McQueen (my co-developer of the content management strategy diagram on page 11), Andrew Gilboy, Eric Hartmann and Anne Rockley for the part they have played in trying to educate me. I would also like to thank the UK e-Information Group (formerly UKOLUG) of CILIP for giving me the opportunity to present seminars on content management that have ended up forming the structure of this book.

Disclaimer

The inclusion of any CMS vendor company in this book is for purposes of illustration and is not to be regarded as a recommendation by the author. The list of CMS vendors on page 81 is likewise an illustration of some of the companies offering products and services in the UK market.

References

Boiko, B. (2002) *Content Management Bible*, New York, Hungry Minds.

Rockley, A, with Kostur, P. and Manning, S. (2002) *Managing Enterprise Content: a unified content strategy*, Indianapolis, New Riders, www.newriders.com.

Martin White

Terms and definitions

Approval   The signing-off of changes as part of a 'workflow' process. *See also* **Workflow**

Asset   The individual elements that are held in a CMS respository are often referred to as assets.

'Baked' publishing
  See **'Static' publishing**.

CMS   This acronym can be used for a range of systems and applications, as discussed in Chapter 1. The general use is as Content Management Software. Because of other uses, such as Client Management System and Case Management System, care is needed to understand the context in which CMS is being used.

Content management system
  A content management system defines the way in which content is managed within an overall content management life-cycle from creation to publication.

Content repository
  The database in which the the documents, pages and other content items are held within a CMS.

Content re-use
  Use of a single piece of content in more than one instance, and in such as way that updating this content also ensures that all instances of its use also link to the revised content.

CSS   Cascading Style Sheets, which enable design elements, such as font type, font size and colours to be specified for web pages.

Digital asset management

Digital asset management (DAM) systems are used to manage non-text content, such as graphics, pictures, images and video clips.

Digital rights management

Digital rights management (DRM) systems enable an organization to manage the intellectual property rights associated with content, in particular copyright and licensing agreements.

Document management system

Document management systems (DMS) manage the creation, revision and distribution of formatted documentents. There is often a requirement to handle documents that the organization receives from outside parties, and to manage scanned documents, such as letters and drawings.

Document Type Definition

Document Type Definitions (DTD) enable XML documents to be interpreted by software so that specific elements (such as a title) are recognized and processed/displayed in an appropriate way.

Dublin Core Metadata

A set of 15 metadata elements that are widely used as the basis for metadata schemes. The Dublin Core Metadata is maintained by OCLC Inc.

Dynamic publishing

The pages of the website or intranet are generated dynamically at the point when they are accessed by site visitors. The CMS assembles the pages from the content stored in the central repository.

ECMS   *See* **Enterprise content management system**.

Enterprise content management system

> An enterprise content management system integrates web content management system, with additional applications sush as document management, records management and digital asset management .

EDMS   Electronic document management system.

EIP   *See* **Portal**.

ERMS   Electronic records management system.

ERP   Enterprise resource planning.

HTML   HyperText Markup Language (HTML).

Information architecture

> Information architecture (IA) consists of process and techniques for determining the structure of the content, including navigation and linking requirements. IA also encompasses metadata and search engine design.

ITT   *See* **Statement of requirements**.

Learning content management system

> A learning content management system (LCMS) is specifically designed to create and manage the content of training and academic courses.

Metadata   Metadata is information about a content asset, such as the name of the author, the date of publication and expiry, the nature of the document (report, press release) and subject keywords that faciliate finding the content.

Personalization

> Portal technology enables a user to define a personalized selection of the information that is presented on their desk top.

Portal   Portal technology enables information from a range of databases and applications to be integrated onto a web desktop. Among these applications could be corporate intranets. They are sometimes referred to as Enterprise Information Portals (EIP).

Records management system

A system that manages the designation, storage and retrieval of documents created, received and maintained by an organization in order to fulfil legal obligations or to provide evidence of a specific business activity.

Repository   *See* **Content repository**.

RFP   *See* **Statement of requirements**.

Statement of requirements

A document that sets out the technical, business and contractual requirements for the procurement of a software product or application. Can also be referred to as an Invitation to Tender (ITT) or Request for a Proposal (RFP).

'Static' publishing

Complete web pages are maintained in the repository and served as required.

TCI   Total Cost of Implementation.

Version control

Any change to a content asset, no matter how small, is designated as a new version of the content, and each of these versions can be listed by the CMS.

WML   Wireless Mark-Up Language.

Wiki   A wiki is a very basic form of content management. It enables groups of users with no HTML experience to create and edit web pages and is increasingly used as a means of supporting collaborative working. The best example is Wikipedia www.wikipedia.com.

Workflow   A process for managing the progress of a document or other content from creation to publication by ensuring that at each stage appropriate checks and approvals have been undertaken.

XML   eXtensible Markup Language (XML).

XSL   eXtensible style language. *See also* **HTML** and **XML**.

1 Creating an information-enabled organization

Introduction

For over three decades, almost without fail, there has been a conference or seminar each year at which librarians and information professionals bemoan the fact that they seem not to be able to break out of their narrow role as information custodians, and have a greater impact on their organization. Their professional knowledge of information management and their practical knowledge of how information is being used (albeit probably ineffectively) in their organization is not being used to its full extent. Organizations rarely have an information strategy, and all the promotion of the business benefits of effective information management is carried out bottom-up because of the lack of a senior sponsor.

Management of websites and intranets

Over the last few years information professionals have started to have a role in the management of websites and intranets, even if somewhat by default as no one else has wanted to take responsibility. This is especially the case with an intranet. As a result, they gave gained new skills, and invariably a higher profile, from their web activities, but still their impact on the organization as a whole is limited. The problem with web technology is that the entry-level cost is very low. All that is needed is a fairly basic PC and some page-authoring software such as FrontPage, and a website can be created at virtually no cost to the organization. Even using more sophisticated page-authoring software such as Dreamweaver adds little to the cost until there is a requirement for training. If the organization has a web server already then starting up an intranet is again almost a zero-cost activity, because the staff costs involved are rarely fully quantified outside of some professional services firms.

Websites

The information content on a website can usually be quite well determined at the point of launch, certainly in terms of the basic structure of the website. The aims of the site are focused on increasing the revenues of the organization, raising awareness and/or providing a service. Over time these may change, but usually in a fairly measured way. There will be a review of the hits on the site, the items downloaded and the position of the site on various search sites and portals. The information content will be added by a small team, whose members will have a good knowledge of what is on the site, and what content needs to be revised or replaced.

Intranets

Intranets are a much greater challenge. Externally it may be business as usual for the organization, but internally there may be frequent and seismic changes to the organization which need to be reflected in the intranet. Two examples from the UK give some indication. In the 2004 Budget the Chancellor of the Exchequer announced that the Inland Revenue and Customs & Excise were to merge. These organizations have thousands of employees in offices throughout the UK, and the problems of integrating their intranets will be quite colossal. Later in 2004 Marks & Spencer replaced their top management team to fight off a hostile take-over bid from Michael Green, and within days changes where announced to the strategy and organization of the retail chain. The e-commerce website of Marks & Spencer will change very little but the company's intranet will be undergoing very substantial change.

Exact figures for the number of intranets in the UK are difficult to obtain, but an estimate of perhaps 300,000 is not far off the mark. However, many large organizations, including universities, still do not have a fully developed intranet. At intranet conferences it tends to be the same intranets that form the speaker roster, and even then the picture that is presented is that the intranet is being heavily used, usually based on the number of hits. The problem is that in the intranet environment hits also mean 'How Idiots Track Success'! Organizations delude themselves that the new intranet is an improvement because the number of hits has increased. The reality may well be that the new design is so bad that employees are using more clicks to find the same information.

The true metric for an intranet is that employees trust it, and trust it to a level of around 99% or more. This means the intranet must provide effective access to reliable and current information, and must also reassure users that when they cannot find a piece of information it is because it is not on the intranet. If there is no trust then users telephone or e-mail colleagues for the information in the first place, rather than use the intranet.

The majority of intranets use the 'webmaster' model, with a small team (often just one person) adding in content supplied in a range of formats and styles by other members of staff. This creates a bottleneck where seniority is everything in jumping the queue to get something published. Then comes the day when a senior manager is seriously inconvenienced and embarrassed by their failure to find something, and they remember reading something in a periodical about the benefits of a content management system (CMS), and start to ask why the organization has not invested in one.

CMS – three letters, many meanings

The problem with the acronym CMS is that there are at least five distinct definitions:

- CMS = content management software
- CMS = content management system
- CMS = contact/client management system
- CMS = case management system
- CMS = complaint management system.

This *Handbook* is about the differences, benefits and risks of content management software and content management systems. The first question to deal with is what is content? A metaphor for this occurred to me when standing on the platform of my local railway station. The first announcement over the loudspeakers was that 95% of trains on the Southern rail network were running to time. That is data. The next announcement was that the train that I was waiting for was running 15 minutes late. That is information. However, I knew that if I caught the train due to leave in five minutes from another platform going to a different destination I could change and catch another train further up the line, and still get to London on time. That is knowledge.

By listening carefully to the announcements it was possible to hear how each one was stitched together from a set of pre-recorded station names, train times and reasons for being late. There was also the three-tone sound at the beginning to alert you to the announcement. That is content. Using a PC the station announcer can quickly make up any announcement from the individual content items, which include a range of sound effects.

It could be said that content is granular information. In the context of a web environment it could include:

- text
- graphics
- pictures
- sounds
- videos
- data.

The aim of content management software is to provide a way of creating pages from a repository of content items, ensuring that any individual item (such as a map of the office location) is stored only once, but can be used in many different pages. Updating the map would then update the version of the map on every page it is used, without the need for the web manager to remember the pages concerned.

Implementing content management software does not necessarily result in a content management system. Indeed it is possible to have a content management system without using content management software. Even more important, without a content management system the chances of content management software working at all are remote. The basis of any system is a set of rules, and many organizations have effective sets of rules for the production of documents. This is especially the case in the pharmaceutical industry, where there is extensive use of standard operating procedures for activities such as clinical trials, and the reports that have to be prepared from the trial data. Law firms have equally strict rules not only on structure and format but on who needs to approve an opinion before it is sent to the client.

In most organizations there are probably a few such standard procedures, with all the other procedures for document preparation being implicit and somewhat variable. Memos and minutes of meetings are examples of where personal and/or departmental preferences come to a very visible surface. This extensive implicit and poorly managed situation presents an enormous challenge to the implementation of content management software because the software needs a set of rules to work by, because computers are in fact very unintelligent. In content management software implementations the old adage of 'garbage in – garbage out' holds absolutely true.

Distributed content authoring

One of the benefits of content management software is that it facilitates the authoring of content by employees with no technical skills in hypertext mark-up language (HTML). Content can be added to the CMS through a text editor with the basic word-processing functionality of Bold, Italic, Underline, Font, etc. The other route is to prepare the document in Word and cut and paste this into the CM software, though this can be fraught with technical problems (see Chapter 2). The overall benefits of this approach should be that content is added to the intranet more quickly, and by people with an interest in ensuring that the content is correct. However, even with the best CM software time is required not only to add the content but also add metadata to increase the chances that the content can be found by others when required. The extra work involved invariably gives rise to the issue that department managers want to know who is going to provide the extra resources they need to add content which is of benefit to the organization as a whole but adds a significant extra burden to the work of the department.

There are some senior managers who see another side of distributed content authoring and that is that staff may post content that is inappropriate to the organization. They are reassured by the CM software vendor that the workflow procedures built into the software will make sure that this never happens. This is not the main justification for developing workflow processes. Staff publishing inappropriate information should be seen as breaching their contract of employment and dealt with appropriately.

Opportunities for the information profession

Most users of Microsoft Office applications do not realize that there is a Properties box that enables them to fill in some basic metadata about the document that they are preparing. The failure to do so is often a source of amusement and competitive intelligence to other organizations who check the box to see which contract has been used as the basis for the one that has been sent. (Turning on Track Changes can also be an education!) Developing appropriate metadata schemas is core to a successful software implementation, and this is where information professionals have a major contribution to make to the successful implementation of CM software.

Within any organization different departments and subsidiaries call things different names. This is especially the case with international organizations. In the UK, Boxing Day is a bank holiday, but Boxing Day is unique to the UK, as is the term 'bank holiday', so how should a document about emergency procedures for Boxing Day 2004 be tagged so that the office in Japan understands that if there is a problem with the IT network on 26 December 2004 they know who to call at home in the UK?

Metadata is closely linked to information architecture and findability. The concept of findability is fairly new, and is largely the creation of Louis Rosenfeld and Peter Morville in their book *Information Architecture for the World Wide Web* (2002). The concept relates to the way that content can be discovered through a combination of effective navigation, hyperlinking and search. Searching is a core area of expertise for the information profession, but is something that is often ignored or downplayed by IT managers when selecting and implementing CM software.

The opportunities for the information profession are much wider than classification and search, with the key role being in documenting the way in which information, and knowledge, is used within the organization through information and content audits. In the past there has been some scepticism of the value of information audits, but in the context of a content management system they are an essential activity. Until an organization understands the content it owns, or acquires from external resources, how can it begin to manage this content?

Digital convergence

Digital technology has blurred traditional media boundaries, and this process needs to be considered in the selection of CM software. Organizations with e-learning resources will probably be using a learning management system (LMS) to track who has taken each course and what scores have been achieved, a process that is increasingly important in industries with strict governance and compliance requirements. Organizations making use of images, video and other content that is subject to copyright may be using a digital rights management (DRM) system and a digital assets management (DAM) system. Then there are Client Management Systems (CMS).

The focus so far in this chapter has been on web-based systems, but much of the content in an organization is in ASCII format within Microsoft Office applications. These may have been incorporated into an electronic document management system (EDMS), which in turn is linked into, or even provides, an electronic records management system (ERMS). An organization may have implemented a human resources (HR) portal to provide staff with access to their personal files and benefits, and this portal may also provide access to HR policies and procedures.

Most organizations are finding that e-mail use is out of control as employees send copies of documents around the office, putting pressure on the recipient to file it, which they do, each in a different location. Then there are instant messaging applications, and blogs and wikis are starting to move inside the firewall.

The IT solution to all this convergence is to promote the deployment of a portal, but this can make the situation worse. A portal is a desktop window on a range of applications, each containing content. The value of a portal is as good as the least reliable information source that is accessible through the portal, because portal technology does not usually provide the tools to create content, only to access content.

The other important convergence is the basis of CM software, and that is the convergence between structured data (sometimes information!) in a database and unstructured text and other information typically held in Microsoft Word and PowerPoint applications. Not only is the volume of unstructured information substantially higher than the structured information, but it may well have a greater value to the organization. Using XML, CM software can create (in effect) a structured repository of unstructured information/content. Then, in the same way that changing an address in a database would ripple through all other relevant data sets (perhaps to allocate the person to a different account executive), changing the office location map would do the same to the website and one or more intranets.

Document and records management

If 'content management' is an ill defined term then the same can also be said for 'document management' and 'records management'. A document is a fixed aggregation of content, so that there is a defined and constant number of pages, for example. A document can also be printed. Many content management products offer document management features, but these almost always relate to the preparation of documents within the organization. A wider view of document management is the ability of the organization to handle documents that are prepared by third parties, and not necessarily in electronic format. These could be forms that have been completed by hand, or handwritten letters sent to the organization. These may need to be scanned in and either managed as scanned files or converted to a digital text format through optical character recognition.

In 2003 the Xerox Corporation commissioned the market research company International Data Corporation to undertake a study of the attitudes of European companies to document management (Xerox Global Services, 2003).

The headline results are:

- 70% believe that poor document process management could impact operational agility
- 82% believe that documents are crucial to the successful operation of their organization
- 97% do not know what percentage of their revenue is spent on documents and 90% could not estimate how much they spend on documentation
- 95% of European organizations are not able to estimate the cost of wasted or unused documents

- 45% of executives' time is spent with documents.

The authors of the report observe that:

> One of the potential barriers that emerge from the research is an ambiguous understanding of what precisely constitutes documentation. While 83%, 78% and 76% consider faxes, email and electronic files as documents, respectively, only 48% and 46% categorise web pages and multimedia content as such.

Xerox defines document management as:

> embracing process, methods, and technologies employed to handle documents throughout their lifecycle – from inception through creation, review, storage and dissemination all the way to their destruction – in ways that will serve an organisation's mission-defined goals and objectives.

This life-cycle approach is the major difference between content management and document management. If what the organization wants is document management then implementing a content management solution is very unlikely to meet the full range or requirements.

Records management takes document management into a further aspect of business process, because records have to be managed within a business process framework so that there is an audit trail for legal and compliance purposes. An important aspect of records management is the disposal of records based on defined retention and disposal policies, and again this is a feature that is currently unlikely to be found within a content management application.

Enterprise content management

One further acronym is ECM. It describes a state of Nirvana where the entire content of an organization is maintained in one repository that lies at the heart of websites, intranets, extranets, document management, records management and all the other digital content management applications referred to above.

In September 2002, Deloitte Consulting published a report

entitled *Enterprise Content Management: taming content chaos* (Deloitte Research, 2002), one of the first reports to look at content from an enterprise perspective. The report states:

> In today's highly competitive and continuously evolving global marketplace, how you manage information will make or break your business. Content management can no longer be regarded as an offshoot of IT. Rather, your content management approach must be indivisible from your company's overall strategy. An intelligent approach to content management integrates content assets and workflows into an overarching enterprise-wide information supply chain that can be adopted by employees, utilised by suppliers and understood by customers.

The challenge for organizations is to decide whether to implement an integrated ECM from one vendor or create an ECM on a modular basis by purchasing what are referred to as 'best of breed' applications from a range of vendors. Although some vendors offer what they see as an ECM solution these solutions are still first-generation solutions that have been built from recently acquired companies. Documentum and Open Text are two such vendors. For an ECM to work there has also to be an enterprise information architecture and, if not an enterprise taxonomy, at least a way of linking together a range of taxonomies and classification schemes, a process made orders of magnitude more difficult by working in more than one language. In this situation American English and British English count as two languages.

However, ECM is still seen as very much the management of operational information, and several vendors, notably Documentum, are promoting the idea of information life-cycle management, which extends from content authoring to records management. Not surprisingly some of the vendors promoting this concept are not software companies but storage companies, keen to sell the next generation of very large computer storage technology. Documentum is in fact owned by ESC, one of the leading storage technology companies.

Developing and implementing a content management strategy

There are more questions than answers so far in this chapter, and they can be answered only in the context of a content strategy statement such as that made by Professor Don Marchand of IMD Business School, Lausanne, in his book *Competing with Information* (Marchand et al., 2000):

> Companies compete with information to the extent that managers and employees seek, collect, organise, process and use the relevant information in decision making and actions that lead to superior business performance. Effective use of information is critical to how executives manage their companies and how businesses create value in their markets.

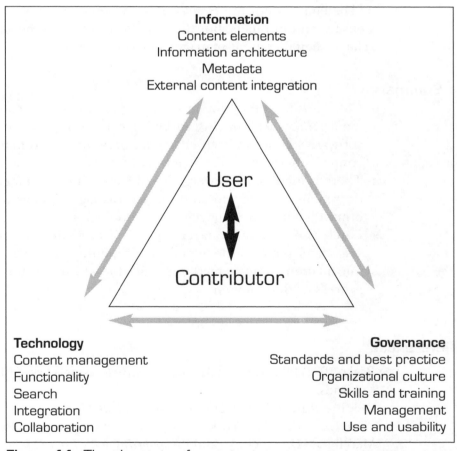

Figure 1.1 The elements of a content management strategy

If content is the building-block of information, and so at least explicit knowledge, then without a content management strategy an organization is going to fail to compete, even if it is with another university or charity. Nowadays not-for-profit organizations are increasingly competitive, be it for the best students or the richest sponsors. Even when (and indeed if) information life-cycle applications do become widely available content management will still be the core of these systems.

This *Handbook* is built around the three elements of a content strategy, which are set out in Figure 1.1 (page 11). The first section covers the information issues; technology options, including how to select CM software are considered next; and finally some governance issues are discussed.

The emphasis of the *Handbook* is on web content management for websites and intranets, but the basic principles are the same for any related digital content management application.

Summary

- CMS can stand for content management *system* and content management *software*. Just installing content management software will not in itself enable an organization to manage content effectively and efficiently.
- There is increasing convergence of web content management, document management and records management, as well as other digital asset management technologies.
- Enterprise content management is still very much at the concept stage, and requires the adoption of an enterprise-level information strategy, methodologies for which are still in the process of development.

References

Boiko, B. (2002) *Content Management Bible*, New York, Hungry Minds.

Deloitte Research (2002) *Enterprise Content Management: taming content chaos*, New York, Deloitte Consulting, www.deloitte.com.

Marchand, D. A., et al. (2000) *Competing with Information*, Chichester, John Wiley.

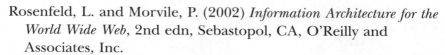
Rosenfeld, L. and Morvile, P. (2002) *Information Architecture for the World Wide Web*, 2nd edn, Sebastopol, CA, O'Reilly and Associates, Inc.

Xerox Global Services (2003) *Documents: an opportunity for cost control and business transformation*, Xerox Corporation, www.xerox.com.

2 Content management functionality

Introduction

This chapter sets out the functionality of content management software. As the CMS industry matures (even though it started only around 1996) most of the products on the market will offer a very similar set of core features. The important thing to recognize is that the way that each product delivers these features, and the inter-relationship between them, can differ significantly. This is why just setting out a list of the desired features in a statement of requirements can result in a failure to meet expectations as the implementation proceeds. The metaphor of a Chinese menu is very apposite. It is easy to ask for quite a number of different dishes and end up with a very unbalanced meal.

As well as understanding what content management software can accomplish it is just as important to understand what the limits are to the technology. Organizations often decide to look for a product that can provide content management, document management and knowledge management within an integrated software suite. These do exist (though with usually limited knowledge management features) but at a price tag that is very high indeed.

A core issue is what is meant by 'document management'. As outlined in Chapter 1, this can range from the ability to manage the collaborative authoring of internal documents to the ability to scan in hand-written letters and forms. Another aspect of document management is the ability to add externally authored electronic documents to a system for internal circulation and eventual storage. This can be important in organizations that need to manage the response of staff to official documents from government and other sources.

Records management can be another grey area. At the time of writing this book the imminent implementation of the Freedom of

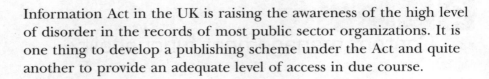

Information Act in the UK is raising the awareness of the high level of disorder in the records of most public sector organizations. It is one thing to develop a publishing scheme under the Act and quite another to provide an adequate level of access in due course.

The impact of XML

One of the important technical advances that has facilitated the development of content management applications is XML, extensible markup language. XML does not replace HTML but complements it. The focus of HTML is on the structure of a document and how it is displayed by a web browser. XML is a database-neutral text language that facilitates the re-use of the content. Like HTML, XML makes use of tags (words bracketed by < and >) and attributes. The difference is that HTML specifies what each tag and attribute means, and often how the text between them will look in a browser; XML uses the tags only to specify pieces of data, and leaves the interpretation of the data completely to the application that is being used. In other words '<h>' in an XML file is not necessarily defining a heading, as it would in HTML.

Unlike HTML, which has a rigid set of rules to mark up content, XML uses a document type definition (DTD) that sets out a specific set of rules that can then be interpreted by extensible style language (XSL). In the example above the definition of '<h>' would be set out in the DTD, but this is still presentation independent. The style sheet is defined by the XSL which renders the content delimited by the <h> parameter as content that should be rendered as 12pt Arial Bold right justified, together with any colour information.

The main benefits of XML are the following:

- XML can be used to store configuration files, attach metadata to documents in a well defined, stable yet extensible format that can be processed using widely available XML tools.
- XML can be used to create documents that can then be used or enriched by various entities in a company.
- XML can be used to exchange data/content between two incompatible databases in a neutral but recognizable (in software) formats.
- XML documents can be published to the web, in Wireless Mark-

up Language (WML) for wireless phones, or even as a printed version.

■ XML can add new elements to an HTML document that will be processed on the server side and rendered in HTML on the web.

As with all technologies there is some associated jargon, and one of the important pieces of jargon relates to the use of 'well-formed' and 'valid'. An XML content item is said to be well formed if there is no associated DTD. An XML document that is conformant to a DTD is said to be valid.

In essence XML enables text to be managed as though it were in a database format, and over the last few years virtually every CMS vendor has become XML-compliant.

Functionality overview

The features that are offered by virtually all content management software products are as follows:

■ content authoring
■ content review
■ content version management
■ content metadata tagging
■ content repurposing for specific audiences
■ comprehensive administration functions.

Content authoring

One of the reasons for an organization to purchase content management software is to try to avoid the bottlenecks caused by having only a few people skilled in the art of HTML publishing. The problems are usually worse in an intranet environment because many of the authors create content only on an occasional basis, and in the period between authoring content find that they have forgotten how to use the page authoring software, especially if it is one of the more powerful and complex packages such as Dreamweaver. The expectation of a CMS is that it will allow staff with little or no HTML authoring knowledge to add content to the site. There are two basic approaches when content is being created for the first time, rather than being adapted from content that is already in the repository.

Templates/text editors

The first of these is to provide a template into which authors can write text and then leave the software to do the formatting. These templates can be just a text notepad area, or provide the author with a WYSIWYG (What You See Is What You Get) editor that offers some of Word-like style elements using familiar icon format, such as Bold, Italic, Bullets, Numbering, etc. Of course templates are not unique to content management software products. Many organizations are already familiar with templates through the use of Dreamweaver, and some vendors will support the migration of these templates into their system. The ease with which templates can be created and modified varies widely between vendors.

Sometimes the very simplicity of this approach can be frustrating for the author, who may want to add a particular feature to make the content more usable but finds that there is no way of doing so. For example, there may be an option to produce a bulleted list, but not a numbered list. Two common requirements are spell checking and link management. Spell checking is implemented in a number of different ways. If the editor is just working in the browser then in-line spell checking (as offered with Word) cannot be delivered, and the content has to be run through a spell checker as a separate operation, adding to the authoring time and often giving rise to some degree of frustration on the part of the author.

There are three technical approaches to providing WYSIWYG features, and these are based around ActiveX controls, Java applets and Dynamic HTML (DHTML). In fact many ActiveX applications also make use of DHTML code.

There can be some accessibility issues with these text editors:

- Staff with visual or other handicaps may find that they cannot use the full functionality of the template, especially if they are using a voice browser.
- The HTML code is very heavily tagged and as such may not be rendered through a voice browser for verification.

Many of the content management vendors buy in their text editors from a specialist supplier. Probably the most popular products are eWebEdit Pro and CMS 200 from Ektron, which is a content management software vendor in its own right. A list of XML-compliant editors can be found at www.xml.com/pub/pt/3. There is a good list of editors, along with browser requirements at www.bris.ac.uk/is/projects/cms/ttw/ttw.html. The browser requirements can be quite stringent, which can give rise to problems in organizations that have content authors in less IT-developed countries of the world, or where there has not been a need for every desktop in the organization to use the latest version of Internet Explorer.

Word file conversion

The second approach is to enable authors to copy and paste in content from a Word file, or another DTP software. This may seem like the ultimate solution because authors will already be familiar with Word. However, transforming a Word document is not just a process of creating a basic HTML file. The Word document itself will have a lot of styling embedded in it, ranging from sub-heading sizes to table layouts, and to transform this to HTML code is not a straightforward matter. There is an implicit assumption on the part of CMS vendors that organizations are able to have absolute control over the style of Word documents. The reality is rather different. Even small differences, such as right-hand justifying a document before adding it to a template that is based on unjustified text, can give rise to some interesting results. Problems also arise when authors have used sections from more than one document, not realizing some subtle differences in the respective style sheets.

Michael Gross, Chief Technology Officer, Data Conversion Laboratory, Inc. provides an excellent overview of the problems that can be encountered in *When Word-XML Conversions Get Nasty* at www. cmswatch.com/Features/TopicWatch/FeaturedTopic/ ?feature_id=98.

Finding and editing existing content

As a website or intranet grows in terms of content it is likely that existing content will need some degree of editing and enhancement to create a content item. The issue of how this content is to be found is an important one to address early in the specification development. There are two common scenarios:

- The first is where the author is going to adapt their own content and, since (in theory!) they know where they stored it in the file folder hierarchy, finding it again can be accomplished though browsing through folders.
- The second scenario is best illustrated by the situation in which an author in Department A wishes to create a policy document based on one developed and published by Department B. Since each author tends to built folder structures in different ways, finding this content can be quite difficult. One approach is to use the built-in search engine that many vendors provide, but this can result in a substantial number of hits that then have to be reviewed on a content item basis. Another approach, often used by lower-cost products, is to provide the ability for authors to modify existing web pages. This seems attractive at first glance, but has some drawbacks. First all that is being edited is the web page, and there may well be a pdf or Word document as well. Second, even if the content can be changed the design will not be editable, which may or may not be a good thing.

Images

One further aspect of content authoring is the way in which the system enables images to be identified, edited, tagged and positioned on the web page. This is quite a complex area, especially as images may require the author to be able to check on licence rights before using the image. Metadata for images are also much more complex because of the variables involved, and this is discussed in more detail in Chapter 3.

Interface

The authoring interface also has to provide a range of access privileges. Access rights can be granted on the basis of:

- the identity of the author, so that John Smith has rights to modify any content on the system
- the authority of the author, so that only the Personnel Manager can add new jobs to the intranet
- the department of the author, so that library staff can access and modify user newsletters.

Forms

On both websites and intranets the ability to provide forms as a way of gathering information is important. In an intranet the use of forms can be a very effective way of creating lists of events and meetings, and of course for websites forms are vital to be able to capture site registration details. Careful attention needs to be given as to how easy forms are to prepare, and also the extent to which the software can be used to validate the information provided.

Link management

An important element of content authoring is the ability to insert and then manage hypertext links. This can be quite a challenge with a website, but for an intranet it becomes a mission-critical functionality because of the dispersed content contribution approach, and also because usually the rate of change of content is higher than at most websites. It is important to understand how an author can select a link in the first place, and then how the system is able to ensure that there are no broken links in the repository.

One of the benefits that a CMS can bring is the ability to do a global change of all links should a link need to be changed. Although a global change is certainly useful it can also be of benefit to see the context for the link, because the text surrounding the link may also need to be changed. It is also useful if the CMS can alert an author to the fact that a page they are proposing to change or delete is linked to other pages, and perhaps prevent them from taking either action until agreement is reached with the author(s) of those other pages.

It is in the area of link management where there are some differences between CMS products, not only regarding when and how a link is validated but even which links can be managed.

Vendors sometimes refer to 'internal' and 'external' link management. In many cases 'external' does not refer to the internet, but to content and links that do not reside on the CMS server itself, but perhaps on a document management system or a customer management system.

Since the basis of web technology is to provide hyperlinks to related pages the extent to which a CMS delivers on this aspect of functionality should be investigated with considerable attention to process and usability.

Creating tables

As many websites illustrate, the constraints on table creation in HTML are considerable. It is in processes such as link management and table creation that CMS vendors can be differentiated. Sometimes only basic table formats are provided, and these can be very limiting. If tables are important to the organization then samples of current tables should certainly be included in the statement of requirements, and demonstrated during the selection process.

Content review

The aim of this process is to enable a piece of content to be created, and then automatically forwarded to another employee for review and/or for approval to publish. However, the first person to review the content will be the author, and it is essential that they are able to look at the content as it will appear on the site with the absolute minimum number of clicks, ideally one!

Review and approval are two different processes which may be combined. A library user newsletter may be written by one member of the library, and forwarded to a colleague for review. The decision to approve the newsletter for publication on the site may need to be taken by a more senior manager. The approval to publish on an intranet may also involve reviewing the circulation of the content. In many situations the two activities may be performed by one person.

As well as reviewing the text of the item there is also a requirement to ensure that metadata have been correctly applied. This requires knowledge of the metadata that a reviewer of the content may not have. If the correct metadata are not applied then the content may be lost to a search engine. Processes for the review of metadata tagging are therefore important, but are inevitably time consuming. It is probably not realistic to expect a content reviewer to comment on metadata, and so some form of sampling of content by the web team is probably required.

Reading content on a screen is not ideal and almost certainly the reviewer will want to print out the content to read it through and for this a colour printer is essential. Having read through the content the reviewer may wish to make some quite important changes. This is usually accomplished with a free-text box on the review screen. Ideally it should be possible to annotate the text along the lines of the Mark Revisions feature on Microsoft Word, but that facility is rare. It should also be remembered that there may be very small changes between successive versions of the same item of content, perhaps just a recropped image or a small change in sentence construction. These changes may not be immediately obvious to the reviewer. All this argues for taking as much effort to specify and assess the review process as the initial process of content authoring.

Workflow

Most organizations understand the concept of workflow, but usually it is implicitly built into the brains of staff and not explicitly set out in software code. Staff know that if Manager A is away then either Manager B or Manager C will look over a report, or the minutes of a meeting. Try building even the most simple of workflows for this and the complexity starts to show. What happens if Manager A is away for the day on business? Will the CM system realize that they have not logged on and automatically transfer relevant information to Manager B, or is there a way of alerting the content contributor to the fact that Manager A is away? In good workflow systems there are many options, but the very fact there are all these options means that setting up the preferred route can take a lot of time and effort.

In the case of intranet workflows the organization may already have a workflow system in place for other applications. This can give rise to problems as the initial content may have been prepared within a case management system used by a law firm, but then needs to be published on the corporate intranet or on the website. Ideally the workflow system for the case management system and for the content management system should be linked, but there can be technical difficulties.

There may be instances where content needs to go outside the organization for review and approval, such as a press release being approved by a PR agency, or content going out for translation. The CMS should be able to cope with sending content to e-mail addresses that are not in the network directory of the organization. This may seem quite easy to do but can give rise to complications as the options for sending content for review may be limited to addresses on the network of the organization.

The effort involved in developing workflows is often not appreciated, and there is also a tendency to try to be too clever with workflow, rather than taking a minimalist approach in the early stages. Managers may see workflow systems as a means of making sure staff do not post inappropriate content on to the intranet, but this is not an effective use of the technology. The posting of inappropriate content should be dealt with under normal disciplinary procedures.

In general workflow applications should be used with discretion. They can be valuable, indeed essential, where there is a legal or regulatory requirement, and especially if the content is to be published on a website at some time in the future.

The basic principle should be that every workflow application should be justified as enhancing the value of the content to the user, and not as a way of 'controlling' content in an authoritarian way. It will be much easier to increase the number of content processes controlled by workflow when the success of the initial processes is visible, and experience has been gained in implementing a workflow.

Content version management

Every time a piece of content is checked out of the repository even the most minor of changes (e.g. a spelling mistake) will result in a new version number being created. A long document that is being developed by a number of authors can therefore quickly build up a very long list of versions, and identifying intermediate versions can be difficult. This is a fundamental functionality of a CMS, and the usual rule is that no piece of content can be checked out by more than one user at a time. There may be a requirement for several authors to be able to work on different sections of the content at the same time. This is more a feature of document management applications than content management applications.

The ability to make easy comparisons between two versions is very useful, but this may result in both versions having to be checked out, and that can have an impact on the access to content. If the version management checks out both items of content, and no changes are made to one version (because it was opened up for reference purposes) then it is important that a new date and version is not assigned, because the chronological sequence will then be a false one.

Version management enables a website or an intranet to be rolled-back to a specific date and time. This is important in many organizations where there is a need to show, for regulatory conformance reasons, what content the intranet held on how to deal with a customer complaint on a given day. Good roll-back functionality will also roll back all the links to internal and external content, and because the entire site is being rolled back all the internal links will still be valid.

Of course all the versions are now present in the repository, so that there is a potential problem when searching the repository and finding multiple hits to different versions of the same content. Sometimes this is important, but more often than not the default needs to be to the current version of the content.

Content metadata tagging

Each piece of content needs to have metadata attached before it is added to the repository. Metadata is discussed in more detail in Chapter 3 but for now it is important to consider how this metadata will be added to the content. There are two basic approaches to metadata addition:

■ Metadata tags are added automatically to content based on a set of rules, usually linked to a particular template. A sales report will automatically have a tag applied to say that indeed it is a 'Sales Report'. The author may automatically be tagged as the person who has logged on to the system, and not only is the name of the author tagged to the content, but also the department name, so that all content produced by, for example, the Sales Department can be found if required.

■ Other metadata must be added through a manual process. This could range from the review date of the content to the subject terms that need to be applied. Again each template could offer only those metadata fields and terms that are appropriate to the content, but even this will result in quite a considerable overhead for each piece of content. Adding metadata can easily double or treble the time taken for content contribution, and this is a process that is often not quantified when basic productivity metrics are developed to make the business case.

If the effort to add the metadata tags is seen by content contributors as onerous and not related to the value created for searching, then metadata tagging will quickly disintegrate and much of the value of the CMS will be lost.

Content publishing and repurposing

In principle CMS software is able to repurpose content automatically to take into account different styles and formats used in a website and an intranet for the same content, and is also to create pdf and other file formats simultaneously. In general there is an emphasis in CMS selection on content contribution, and not enough on working through how publishing will be managed.

There are two approaches to the way in which content is served up into a browser:

■ The first of these serves static pages and so only requires the use of a web server. This is also referred to as static rendering. When a page is requested the CMS looks at the cache of pages and sends the requested page to the browser for display. This usually makes for fast delivery of pages, but can give rise to problems where the site is updated regularly, as the caching may not be current. This approach does enable a copy of the cache to be distributed to a number of servers without requiring an additional copy of the CMS software.

- The second approach is through the dynamic creation of pages. The system selects an appropriate display template and then assembles the elements of the page from tagged components in the repository before presenting the page in the browser. This ensures that the page is as current as possible, but it does require the use of an application server on top of the web server. It is this approach that enables a user to modify a page by calling up the page and making the required changes on the page itself.

Although the ability to provide the latest version of content can be appealing there are some issues with dynamic publishing. The first is that the process of building up the page can take time and server resources, especially if there is a need to obtain data from databases that are not running on the web server itself. The delay may not be long but may still be perceptible, especially if there are pages that are used at the same time every day, such as meeting room availability. Search engines spidering websites have some difficultly with dynamic sites, and there can be some significant problems in implementing web statistics packages.

Speed of publication

An important aspect of publishing is how quickly new pages can be added to the site. A number of issues need to be considered:

- Some CMS systems will not allow pages to be added to the site without a complete rebuild of the site. This can substantially slow down the authoring process and, depending on the server configuration if the pages are published direct to the production server, then the overall performance of the site will be reduced.
- The second issue is whether content can be stored and then published on a defined date in the future.

There is a half-way house. Creating pages in this way is sometimes referred to as 'frying' the pages. Some CMS products enable pages to be 'baked' or preassembled from the database. This process could be carried out on specific sections of the repository. The benefit is that it reduces the workload on the application server, but at the expense of perhaps not being sure that the page served up is in fact the current page.

Other benefits

Another aspect of repurposing is the ability to take one content item and publish it in a number of different ways. A policy document could be published as a pdf so that the integrity and design are optimized for a specific purpose. An HTML version makes it easier to navigate using hyperlinks and is usually a smaller file size, but has no page breaks or page numbering. An rtf or Word file enables a user to be able to take sections of the document and use them to create new documents with the minimum of effort.

As with any aspect of CMS implementation it is advisable to plan ahead and work through not only what might be required to support current business needs, but what the longer-term web strategy is. It may be wiser to invest in functionality at the outset and not use it immediately than have to either add expensive new modules or even move to a new CMS system.

Content replication

In the case of organizations that have operations around the world it may well be advisable to replicate the site (especially in the case of an intranet) to a number of different servers. This enables the intranet to be accessed over a high-speed network within the office rather than rely on an internet connection which may be working at only 1% of the speed of the office network. The situation may be more complex than this, with a core of content being replicated on a number of different servers, but with local content (perhaps in local language) integrated with the core content.

This will require a very careful assessment of the network and server environment which addresses not only the optimum current scenario but also takes into account planned expansion or contraction of the global office network.

Site structure and design management

Although much can be accomplished with cascading style sheets

(CSS) in terms of creating new designs and layouts for a website the options within a CMS are usually more powerful. This does not mean that no attention needs to be paid to information architecture issues at the outset, as the tagging of the elements needs to be carried out in order to facilitate future redesign, and in any case the CMS will publish to a design framework rather than provide a significant amount of graphic design capability within the software itself.

There is a fallacy that a CMS enables an organization to make quite dramatic changes to the look and feel of the site, including a radical change of the information architecture, at virtually the touch of a button. This is a very dangerous assumption. A CMS can implement a site architecture but the tools to create the structure in the first place may be quite limited. One of the initial questions to ask a vendor is how the site structure is presented to the user, and how this site structure is then rendered as a navigation system.

A requirement in intranet work is often the ability to move a set of pages from one section of the site to another section of the site, perhaps because a department has changed its responsibilities, and all pages relating to training have to be transferred from Human Resources to a new Training Department. This will require the addition of a new section to the site, and the transfer may be a substantial number of pages, along with all the associated hyperlinks. This is the type of operation that may have to be undertaken on a regular basis with an intranet, but which is usually skipped over in vendor selection.

The way to work through these issues is to look back at changes that have been carried out on the current site (or would have been carried out if the technology had been available!) and work through how this process can be carried out in the potential CMS products. Real-world examples from your organization are more revealing than the pre-packaged demonstrations that vendors give in their two-hour presentations.

Comprehensive administration functions

These are especially valuable in a decentralized content contribution situation to enable reports to be produced indicating content that has not been updated, or to allocate content from a specific contributor who has left the organization to another employee. Other important aspects of the administration capabilities are the management of document security and the ability to design new templates. Most CMS products provide an almost endless array of administration capabilities, so it is important to bear in mind that only a relatively few of these are required on a regular basis.

It is through the administration functions that access rights are managed, and this area is perhaps one that is new to an organization investing in a CMS to facilitate distributed content contribution.

Summary

- The basic functional elements of content management software are content authoring and review, content management supported by metadata tagging, content publishing and content administration.
- All CMS products offer these functions, but do so in different ways, so it is very difficult to compare products on the basis of the functional elements alone.
- CMS selection has to be driven by a clear understanding of how implementing a CMS will have a direct benefit on organizational performance.

3 ▪▪▪▪ Information architecture and metadata

Introduction

The implementation of a CMS tends to bring the concepts of information architecture and metadata to the centre of the stage. Both information architecture and metadata are linked together in the quest to achieve websites and intranets that provide users with an intuitive path to the information they are seeking. Another facet of usability is findability, a concept developed by Peter Morville (http://findability.org):

> the quality of being locatable or navigable. At the item level, we can evaluate to what degree a particular object is easy to discover or locate. At the system level, we can analyze how well a physical or digital environment supports navigation and retrieval.

Findability and usability are not the same, but are closely related. Morville also comments that:

> Information architecture is a discipline concerned with the structural and semantic design of shared information spaces. Findability is a goal of IA, along with usability, desirability, credibility, and accessibility.

Information architecture

Information architecture crept into existence in the late 1990s but it was not until the publication of the book *Information Architecture for the World Wide Web* by Louis Rosenfeld and Peter Morville in 1998 that the term became widely used. In the second edition of their book Rosenfeld and Morville (2002) suggest the following definitions:

1 the combination of organisation, labelling and navigation schemes within an information system

2 the structural design of an information system to facilitate task completion and intuitive access to content

3 the art and science of structuring and classifying web sites and intranets to help people find and manage information

4 an emerging discipline and community of practice focused on bringing principles of design and architecture to the digital landscape.

There is no accepted definition of 'information architecture', and that is a good thing at this stage of its development. (The same problem befell 'information science', which dates from the mid-1950s and still has no widely agreed definition.) In 2002 the Asilomar Institute for Information Architecture (www.aifia.org) was set up in the USA. It offers the following definitions of information architecture:

■ the structural design of shared information environments
■ the art and science of organizing and labelling websites, intranets, online communities and software to support usability and findability
■ an emerging community of practice focused on bringing principles of design and architecture to the digital landscape.

Rosenfeld and Morville give the following reasons for the importance of effective information architecture:

■ **The cost of finding information** – If the intranet or website is poorly organized, users waste time (and indeed may give up) trying to find information that they are certain should be on the site.
■ **The cost of not finding information** – If a decision is made on the basis of incorrect information because the correct information cannot not be found on the site, then the costs to the organization can be substantial.
■ **The cost of construction** – Websites and intranets are expensive to create, so approaches are needed to ensure that there is the closest possible match between user requirements and site deliverables at the outset.

- **The cost of maintenance** – Even with a good initial site the organizational objectives will change, as will the information requirements, and these need to be reflected in the site with the minimum of effort and disruption.
- **The cost of training** – The more intuitive the site the lower the training costs, not only at the launch of the site but on an ongoing basis as new employees join the organization. This training cost also applies to employees who have to use the web design applications to add or edit content.

The essence of information architecture is probably best summed up in a poster devised by Victor Lombardi and Dan Willis:

Information architecture is the art and science of organizing and labeling websites, software, intranets, and online communities to support usability and findability. Creating solid information architecture requires researching user needs and testing solutions with users. This puts the user at the core of development and leads to products that delight customers. Good information architecture results in:

- Products that are easier to use
- Information that is easier to find and understand
- Higher customer satisfaction (which can lead to higher sales). (http://aifia.org/tools/download/IAforBiz-AndTech_8.5x11.pdf)

Information architecture and content management

The connection between information architecture and content management is that a content management system facilitates the development of websites and intranets that provide an intuitive path for the user to the information they are seeking. Websites and intranets have grown up on the basis that one-size-fits-all, and that there is nothing wrong with making the user work to find the information they want. The result is a site that has not only a compromise structure to accommodate all users to a 50% satisfaction level but is unable to make changes because of the complexity and time that is required to rebuild the site.

The adroit implementation of a CMS should enable the

organization to provide a high degree of customization for users so that key user communities feel that the site has been designed expressly for them. The reality is that much of the content is common to a number of different sections of the site, but with a CMS the content can be added to the repository once and can then be reused in a number of different ways.

Usability

The principles of usability, like information architecture, have also crept slowly on to the stage. If Rosenfeld and Morville's book was an important catalyst for the acceptance of information architecture then *Designing Web Usability* by Jakob Nielsen (1999) performed the same function for usability when it was published. Interestingly there is only a passing mention of information architecture in the book, which is an indication of the limited awareness of information architecture in 1997/8 when Nielsen was writing his book.

Yet only a few years later Nielsen was writing this in the introduction to the second edition of Rosenfeld and Morville's book (Rosenfeld and Morville, 2002):

> Usability is an important, though not the only, determinant for the success of a website or an intranet. Information architecture is an important, though not the only, determinant for the usability of a design. There are other issues as well, yes, but ignore information architecture at your peril. Critics may say that users don't care about information architecture: they don't want to learn how a website is structured. Users just want to get in, get their task done, and get out. Users focus on tasks, not on structure. I think that it's exactly because users don't care about the structure of a website that it is so important to get the information architecture right in the design. Since we know that users won't spend time learning our information architecture, we have to spend resources to design the best information architecture we can.

The challenge for the web team is to create paths through the website that meet the requirements of core groups of users. If these paths can be established and implemented (and assuming that the content is relevant and current) then user satisfaction will be significantly enhanced. The first task is to develop the paths, and for this the use of personas is being increasingly widely recognized as an effective methodology (Pruitt and Grudin, 2003).

Creating an information architecture through personas

A persona is a real virtual user! The person described in the persona does not actually exist but is created through research to typify some of the characteristics of a group of users. Biographical details are developed, even down to a photograph, so that the person concerned is so real that the web team or intranet team starts to identify with them as an individual member of staff of the organization or as a visitor to the website.

The main characteristics of personas are as follows:

- Personas are hypothetical archetypes, or 'stand-ins' for actual users that drive the decision making for interface design projects.
- Personas are not real people, but they represent real people throughout the design process.
- Personas are not 'made up'; they are ideally discovered as a by-product of the investigative process.
- Although personas are imaginary, they are defined with appropriate rigour and precision.
- Names and personal details are made up for personas to make them more realistic.
- Personas are defined by their goals.

The benefits of using personas are as follows:

1 Websites, like all good software projects, work best when they provide the level of interactive response that you might get from asking a person. This is directly appealing to the human mind, which seeks information in a series of steps through conversation, and not through ploughing through all available resources. A library would be much easier to run if the books were shelved in author sequence, not in subject sequence. But even with subject sequences there is always a heavy use of the help desk to help the user focus in on specific needs.

2 Personas enhance the project management of web development, as each persona becomes a specific project, and a personalized one. The experience at an organization such as the BBC is that the team responsible for the Jane persona really starts to think like Jane, and is clear about the scope of the Jane project.

3 Above all personas ensure that the website focuses on the needs of real people, and not convenient (from the organization standpoint) groups.

4 They provide the basis for the usability testing that is carried out throughout the development of the site.

■■■
■
Personas – a case study
■

The same techniques can be used for an intranet but for the purposes of illustration I focus on a website example related to the relaunch of the website of the University of Cardiff.

Here is a persona for someone who might be using the university website in the near future:

John is 18 and lives with his parents Elaine and Michael and his elder sister in Harrogate. He is now starting to think about going to University in October 2005. His sister, Sally, is 22 and is in the final year of a degree in Glass Technology at the University of Sunderland. John has an interest in computers, but is also a keen sportsman and has taken part in the UK Junior Short Course Championships in the past. He runs in half-marathons on behalf of Cancer Research. He is thinking about taking a gap year after college and travelling to the Far East, perhaps Vietnam, as he speaks good French from the years his parents spent in France. He hopes to get good A levels in Mathematics, Physics and Music, and has an A/S in Psychology. John enjoys going to classical music concerts and also likes garage music.

The first step is to develop the goals that John has in seeking information. These are often divided into personal, practical and false goals.

Personal goals

- To gain a good university education, but currently John has no specific career ambitions. He might well consider at least a Masters after his initial degree.
- To build on his interest in computing, but perhaps not lose sight of his interest in music.
- To develop his skills as a swimmer and perhaps take part in new athletic activities (such as fencing) that are not easily available in Harrogate.
- To undertake a course that might enable him to study abroad, and perhaps make good use of his French.

Practical goals

- To make sure he finds the university that can meet as many of his current personal goals.
- Not to have to spend too much time doing the research because college life is hectic, and he has a lot of outside interests.
- Does not want the difficulty of having to find accommodation, and wants to be in a university where the halls of residence are close to the campus.
- Wants to be fairly close to good cultural events.

False goals

- Wants to have fun.
- His sister hates her course and her university – wishes she was somewhere else.

The next step is to take the practical goals and start to convert them into questions and answers: this will start to define the navigation/architecture. There are two approaches that can be used, scenarios and walk-throughs.

A scenario

John's tutor has heard that the University of Cardiff will be expanding over the next few years because of the merger with the Medical School. As Cardiff is also the leading centre for research,

John feels that it might be an interesting university to attend. John does not know much about Cardiff, and even before looking at the courses he wants to find out just what the merger might mean. He wants to ensure that his education and outside interests can be met. When he comes onto the site he wants to see immediate assurances about the future of the University. What he sees reassures him, so now he wants to look at courses. He has an interest in computers, but perhaps there are courses that have a heavy reliance on computer technology. These could be in engineering, or even in medical areas, such as diagnostic imaging. He puts computers and music into the 'What are your subject interests' box and finds that Cardiff has courses in engineering, computer science, radiology and music, all with a strong computing background.

A walk-through

John clicks on the box 'Cardiff – the total learning experience' which gives him the key facts about the new University and the way in which the University and the City provide a unique combination of education and personal development. The page links to

'What are your interests?' John enters Computing, Music. In response to 'What A levels do you expect to get?' John then enters Mathematics, Physics and Music.

The website then offers John a selection of courses that meet his interests and his A levels, and provides a list of these, along with an indication of the A level entry requirements.

Music technology – A in Music and two Bs

Radiology – A in Physics, A in Maths, and one other A level. ■■■

How many personas?

The question that is always raised about personas is how many there should be. 'Surely we need more than one, and in the case of a University there may be several dozen?'

This is where the top-level architecture of the site comes into play. The aim is to present a home page that accommodates an agreed number of personas, so that with the first click a visitor is taken to a Level 2 site that is clearly constructed around an individual persona. However, it is impossible to do this for more than around seven to ten personas, because the home page gets too 'busy'. The rest of the home page links to what is agreed is common information. This might be location, weather (!), the history of Cardiff, etc.

The result in website terms is that people feel that designers of the website 'know' what they are looking for, and how they will search for information. This makes them feel comfortable that the effort they will put into the search process will be rewarding at an emotional level and at a practical level, and then there is a 'bonding' with the organization that has set up the website or intranet.

Metadata

Metadata is at the heart of a content management system and the way that it is implemented in a CMS has a very significant impact on the extent to which content can be found and reused. The emphasis is often on getting content into a repository with little thought given as to how it can be retrieved either by the end-user of the site or by a content author looking for existing content on which to build.

There are four broad categories of metadata:

- **Structural metadata** describe the information architecture of the document. These metadata elements might include Title, Summary, Image, etc. Using these elements it is possible to search for a keyword that is in a summary but which is not mentioned in the title of the document. They also relate sections of a report to the overall report.
- **Content metadata** provide a way of identifying documents that may contain relevant subject information. This is usually what most people think about when the word metadata is mentioned.
- **Descriptive metadata** enable the type of document to be identified. In this way a search can be limited to web content, streaming video, etc.
- **Administrative metadata** identify the relationship of the document to the business context. These metadata include, for example, the person and department owning the document, the date when the document is checked for relevancy, and the language of the document.

Probably the most widely used metadata scheme is the Dublin Core scheme (http://dublincore.org/documents/dces/). See Table 3.1.

Table 3.1 Elements of the Dublin Core scheme

Dublin Core	Comment	Category
Title	Ideally needs to be a useful title, and not just Sales Report	Structural
Creator	The person who 'owns' the content of the document/page and has responsibilities for keeping it current and relevant	Administrative
Subject	Often a set of keywords from a taxonomy and/or thesaurus	Content
Description	Could be used to distinguish an organizational chart from an internal report	Structural
Publisher	Could be the departmental web master	Administrative
Contributor	Might enable multiple authors to be linked to a piece of content	Administrative
Date	There are many options for date, such as • date of publication • date for review of the content • date for the expiry of the content	Administrative
Type	Could be used to differentiate between a formal presentation and an internal presentation	Descriptive
Format	Often used for file formats, so that Excel or PowerPoint files can be identified	Descriptive
Identifier	Might be the internal file number of a report	Administrative
Source	Could indicate that the content item is derived from another document, perhaps as a synopsis	Structural
Language	Important in multinational organizations	Structural
Relation	Could show that a content item is a later version of an earlier piece of content	Structural
Coverage	Could be used for both geographic coverage and for temporal coverage	Content
Rights	The content item might be a published paper and there could be a copyright issue	Administrative

One of the objectives of metadata at this level is to deal with a search enquiry such as:

I need to find the PowerPoint presentation [Format] that was developed for the sales pitch [Type] that we used for the Waterloo Station [Subject]. Project [Identifier]. I think that Sheila Clark [Contributor] did a lot of work on it based on the work she did for the Manchester Airport project [Source].

Another benefit of metadata is that search engines can be pointed at specific fields ('I only want documents which have "Dublin" in the title') and the outputs can be set so that each hit is shown as Title + Description in reverse Date order.

Most content management applications support the Dublin Core set, ensuring that content tagged with the Dublin Core set is in effect platform independent. There is also the e-Government Metadata Standard, which is an extended version of Dublin Core for use in UK Government and associated applications (www.govtalk.gov.uk/schemasstandards/metadata_document.asp?docnum=872).

A development strategy for information architecture and metadata

The work on defining an information architecture, and establishing the needs for metadata, needs to be carried out at the very outset of defining the requirements for the software. Neither can be developed in isolation from the business objectives of the organization. The sequence should be as follows:

1 Defining the business objectives confirms the information requirements of the organization.
2 The information requirements must be specified in terms of how users will wish to find information, and this helps to define the content metadata in particular. The organization may work in an environment in which there is a schema for content metadata.
3 Once the structure for the content metadata has been developed the need for taxonomies and classification schemes to develop subject-level metadata can be ascertained.
4 This content has to be written by authors, and then reviewed and approved, leading to a definition of workflow and the requirements for structural and descriptive metadata at the level of an individual item of content. However, the templates used for this metadata also have to accommodate content metadata.
5 The repository of content then has to be managed and this requires the addition of administrative metadata.

Although presented here as a linear process the reality is that there must be continuous iteration between the various processes listed.

One of the main reasons for this is the need to keep an appropriate balance between the effort involved in adding metadata and the potential benefit to the user.

Resourcing metadata tagging

The time it takes for an author to add metadata should never be underestimated. There may well be authors who are adding content to a website or to an intranet on a daily basis, and they will become very familiar with the metadata entry processes. However, there will also be authors who only add content on a very infrequent basis. The effort that they have to put into adding metadata has to be carefully assessed to avoid the situation where almost any metadata is added just to get the content into the repository.

One of the issues to consider is whether the reviewer/approver of a piece of content is able to review not only the content but also the metadata.

Summary

- Implementing a CMS does not mean that the site can be designed after the CMS has been installed.
- Careful consideration must be given at the outset to developing an information architecture that meets user requirements, so that appropriate metadata tagging can be applied.
- Using personas can be a very useful methodology in developing an information architecture, metadata schemes and usability tests.

References

Nielsen, J. (1999) *Design Web Usability*, Indianapolis, New Riders Publishing.

Rosenfield, L. and Morville, P. (2002) *Information Architecture for the World Wide Web*, 2nd edn, Sebastopol, CA, O'Reilly and Associates Inc.

Pruitt, J. and Grudin, J. (2003) *Personas: practice and theory*, http://research.microsoft.com/coet/Grudin/Personas/Pruitt-Grudin.pdf.

4 Developing a content management strategy

Introduction

The basic principles of implementing a content management system are independent of whether the objective is to support a website or an intranet, or both. However, the development of a content management strategy and an associated business case will be different in the two cases. An intranet has a known audience who have information requirements that are scoped by the business objectives of the organization, but it is not the sole source of this information and there are often other IT systems that employees use (such as an HR portal or a customer management system) in conjunction with the intranet. For a website far less is known about the audience outside some broad demographics, for example geographic location and a need to locate a doctor or dentist. Indeed a major justification of a website is to attract to it, and thus the organization, people who are currently unknown to the organization.

Website

Over the last few years there has been a welcome and long-overdue shift from seeing a website as a repository of information that the organization thinks would be useful to a visitor to seeing a website through the eyes of the user, and enriching the user experience. Out of this has come, gradually, the recognition of the importance of information architecture.

All too often little thought is given to categorizing 'visitors'. Instead the website home page creator either makes the assumption that all visitors have identical information requirements, or, because the organization has no idea about the identity of visitors to the site, presents all conceivable options on the home page.

It is important to recognize that a CMS delivers only content.

The design of the site has to be developed by the organization, and from this design comes the style templates that are used to publish the information from the CMS onto the web browser. Whether in a web or an intranet application a thorough understanding of the range of templates required both to capture content at the authoring stage and to present the content at the publishing stage is of critical importance. Although some changes can be made post-implementation it should not be assumed that these changes are easy to make. As with everything else in CMS implementation work that is put in to defining requirements will pay huge benefits in the speed and effectiveness of the implementation.

One of the most effective ways of addressing the visitor segmentation issue is to develop personas and scenarios for the way in which priority groups of users will use the site. The development of personas is described in Chapter 3.

Intranet content requirements strategy

In general websites are subject to fairly continuous review, if only because the organization is able to track the level of use of a website through monitoring page usage. This might not be the best way to monitor the value of a website but it is much better than the level of understanding that most organizations have of their intranet.

Audit of information use

The only way to build up the requisite level of knowledge to review an intranet is to undertake an audit of the way in which information is used within the organization as it will have an impact on CMS implementation. This has to be carried out through a series of individual interviews with everyone from directors down to key operational staff. This is a major commitment of time and resources, but if the organization is not willing to invest in the audit then arguably it is not ready to invest in a CMS, with all the costs and cultural changes that will result (Wood, 2004).

One of the objectives of this audit is to understand the way in which information flows around the organization. The reason for this is that only through an understanding of these flows will it be possible to develop the workflows and administrative metadata that are at the core of a content management system (see Chapter 5).

At this stage the scope is only at quite a high level in terms of the detail of the content. Once the business case has been accepted and work started on a statement of requirements (see Chapter 9) then a page/file level audit of content can be undertaken to support the statement of requirements, especially in regard to the migration of legacy content into the CMS. This is covered in Chapter 12.

An outline interview format is given in Table 4.1.

Table 4.1 Outline interview format

Issue	Comments
What are the business objectives of the department?	
What are most important business processes that the department originates or takes part in?	The aim is to focus in on some key processes, because this also highlights workflow issues.
What are the information requirements that support these processes, and does this information come from: • within the department? • other departments? • the knowledge and expertise of individuals? • sources external to the organization?	This is probably the first time that the department has thought through these information management issues!
What formats does this information come in (reports, forms)?	Format problems are especially prevalent when integrating information from external sources into internal documents.
What is the balance between the department being sent this information and searching it when required?	This question again looks at workflow issues, and also explores whether documents are identified by date, author, title, document number, etc.
How do you find this information if you do not know exactly where the current version is stored?	The issue here is that of the 'current version'. This should be one of the benefits of a content management system.
How are documents and other content created in your department?	It is essential to understand who actually creates the documents, and who reviews them, because it is these processes that need to be managed within the CMS, and within the workflow.

(*Continued on next page*)

Table 4.1 (*Continued*)

Issue	Comments
Which other departments use information you create, and how is this information communicated?	All too often departments have only a vague idea of how information they produce is actually used.
Does your department have formal standards for documents?	This could be in terms of Word style sheets, the way that paragraphs are numbered, the degree of consistency regarding sub-headings, etc.
What legal, regulatory and policy constraints are there on the way that information is handled by the department?	These questions start to address physical and electronic records management requirements, which are at the basis of Freedom of Information legislation (in the UK) and corporate governance requirements.
What levels of document security and confidentiality are implemented?	These will need to be managed within the CMS.
What IT applications are being used?	There could be a contact management system or a project management system – key applications that must be addressed in terms of integration.
What would be the impact on department staff if a new content authoring system was introduced?	Change management can be a major issue.

Content management strategy issues

In this section some of the issues that must be addressed in a content management strategy are set out. Without this level of understanding of the information and document management environment in the organization, developing a specification for a CMS cannot be accomplished without significant risk. The purpose of the audit is not only to establish technical criteria for selection but also to understand the organizational and cultural changes that may have to be achieved ahead of the implementation of the CMS itself.

Organization objectives

The business objectives of the organization for the next two to three years should be set out, including key success factors. Even if the decision to implement a CMS is taken immediately the business case is accepted it will almost certainly take nine to twelve months to fully implement a CMS in any organization. It is therefore important that the CMS business case reflects, as far as possible, the business requirements at least two years ahead to avoid the danger that a short-term problem is identified as the critical success factor, when by the time the CMS is implemented this problem has, by default, been solved.

Information requirements

Those information requirements which will have a specific impact on meeting the business objectives should be set out, together with the associated business processes/workflows. The section should include both information generated from within the organization, and information coming from the organization. Differentiation should be made between explicit (documented) information and implicit information (the knowledge of staff). In a consulting business this could mean ensuring that there is rapid dissemination of project progress reports, or, for a trade association, reports on discussions with relevant agencies.

User segmentation

Each organization has many user segments, such as:

- research and administration
- headquarters and subsidiaries
- people with language and culture differences
- staff working away from an office
- customers and suppliers.

The main user segments, their size, and information requirements should be summarized. It is important to identify important flows of information between the main user groups and/or between departments. One of the problems with many intranets is that they become stores of documents, and do not facilitate the transfer of information.

Often one department has to do a lot of repurposing work on a document from another department to ensure that it can be used effectively. I came across a case where a finance department sent out financial reports to project managers as pdf files generated from Excel spreadsheets, which the project managers then used to enter data into their Excel spreadsheets! Changing the file format to Excel saved all concerned not only a considerable amount of time but also ensured that there were no errors in the information held at project level.

Information technology infrastructure

This section needs to be in an understandable text format, and should not make ill-considered use of the IT architecture charts so beloved by IT managers. It can become too long in proportion to the rest of the document, so setting out a standard of no more than half a page for each subheading is generous.

The topics that need to be covered are:

- information systems architecture
- local and wide area networks
- operating systems
- database environment
- storage environment
- portal implementation
- desktop environment
- e-mail and other messaging
- web environment (intranet/extranet/website)
- current and future browser-based applications
- standards
- outsourcing policy
- training and support
- disaster recovery
- network security.

Anticipated changes to the IT infrastructure over the next two to three years should be summarized.

Systems integration

Requirements for integration of document and content

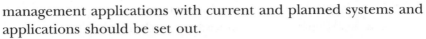

management applications with current and planned systems and applications should be set out.

These would typically include:

- e-mail and other network applications
- personnel systems (excluding payroll)
- enterprise resource planning (ERP) systems
- enterprise information portal (EIP) systems
- records management systems.

The integration requirements should be stated in terms of information exchange, and not in technical terms at this stage. An understanding of the timetable for decision and implementation of new or replacement business applications is especially important. This is because the need to integrate the CMS with these applications (such as a learning management system) may have an impact on the specification of both the CMS and the learning management system. In addition, rolling out two new applications at the same time may cause substantial problems with training and support.

Capital and operating budgets

The basis for the establishment, monitoring and review of capital and operating budgets should be set out: these processes might have an effect on the procurement of the CMS. There have been situations where there has been budget allocated to the purchase of software but no allocation for the professional services required to implement the CMS. Committed and discretionary spending should be identified: sometimes apparent budget flexibility is in fact constrained by the need to upgrade a core system. One of the issues with CMS implementation is that the costs may well extend over one budget year, and yet there is often no way that spending in the following year can be authorized at the time the decision to purchase the CMS is made.

Document analysis

In this section a broad quantification of the document environment should be set out. This will include, for example:

- simple and compound documents
- sequential and collaborative authorship
- document volumes (by above categories)
- rate of change of these volumes
- typical life cycles
- quality management and review.

The timing of specific events (such as an AGM, or a major conference) should be set out, and the short-term impact on document types and volumes should be assessed. In the process of implementation much more work will be needed on document types, but even at this stage some sense of the scale of document diversity and volume is essential.

Document creation

This section should set out in more detail the way in which documents are currently created, for example:

- how many people are typically involved in document creation, review and production
- how often documents are updated and the extent of this updating
- the extent to which a document is a revision of an earlier version or is created from scratch
- existing workflows, which may be implicit rather than documented
- the extent to which documents are used across business processes, and what (if any) repurposing is carried out.

Be prepared for some interesting discoveries in developing an understanding of document creation. The focus on documents rather than 'content' at this stage is deliberate. Many organizations fail to understand the difference between content management applications and document management applications, and as a result purchase a CMS when they really need an EDMS.

External document management

Many documents are received by the organization in printed, written or other formats (video, audio, etc). Other examples include third-party translation of documents. The range of formats should be set out, and the level of integration with internal documents should be analysed. One of the benefits of a document management system can be the management of external documents where there is a need to collate comments and respond to the external agency concerned.

Document publishing

All to often with content management systems the emphasis is on content contribution, and content publishing is not reviewed in sufficient detail. Because some CMS products are better at content contribution than content publishing understanding the publishing requirements is an important consideration in the selection process.

Documents can be published through a number of channels, including, for example:

- as e-mail attachments
- as e-mails addressed to individuals or groups
- posted to an intranet or extranet
- posted to a website
- published in a printed format
- published on CD-ROM/DVD
- circulated in a paper format
- added to a database for internal and external access
- accessed through mobile devices.

The current and anticipated future balance between these (and other channels) should be considered. For example, the implementation of a customer management system (also confusingly with the acronym CMS!) may result in documents relating to specific customers or projects being published through this system.

Security and confidentiality

Documents that should not be accessible to groups of staff within the organization should be identified, together with reasons for the security requirements, and the circumstances under which these restrictions will be lifted (e.g. after a specific period of time). Building a security model for document management needs considerable care at the outset of the implementation, and changing it subsequently can be difficult.

Metadata standards and taxonomies

Metadata issues are covered in more detail in Chapter 3, but at this stage the aim is to understand the current situation and likely requirements, such as:

- extent of current metadata schema
- conformance to Dublin Core and other metadata standards (e.g. e-Government)
- status of taxonomies and classifications
- procedures for updating and revising metadata and taxonomies
- use of computer-based methods for taxonomy creation
- organizational skills to create and maintain metadata schemes.

Search

I have commented above on the concentration on content contribution at the expense of content publishing, and the same is true of content search. The problem is made even worse by the uninformed view of 'All we need is Google'. Certainly Google is a very good search site, but the enterprise version is a rather different product. It may be very difficult to gain an idea of how users will search for information, especially if there is no current search facility on an intranet, but even basic information is valuable, because it may help to understand the scale of the search problem. A search engine can also be a valuable content integrator across a number of different content servers, and in this connection understanding search requirements is essential.

The main types of search that need to be carried out on document/content repositories should be discussed, including:

- approaches to relevance ranking
- document content presentation
- personalization of the results.

The focus should be on how the results should be presented, rather than how the search itself will be carried out. From an understanding of the outputs an indication can be gained of the level of metadata tagging that needs to be applied in order to facilitate this type of output. For example, if a user wants to see the description of a document displayed then the description has to have a field of its own and be tagged accordingly.

Records management

Relevant records management standards and guidelines should be set out, and the extent to which the organization has to meet national or other records retention and management standards should be highlighted. In the UK, Freedom of Information and Data Protection Acts requirements should also be included. One of the issues in many organizations is that records management is still seen as just a way of ensuring that there is a record of all the documents in cardboard boxes in the basement storage area. In the UK there is a wealth of guidance available on records management from the Public Records Office (www.nationalarchives.gov.uk/). The European Commission has sponsored the development of Model Requirements for the Management of Electronic Records (MoReq, www.cornwell.co.uk/moreq).

Governance

This section should set out the organizational structures for managing information flows, including the setting of standards for document and records management. In the UK organizations with registration under ISO 9000 for quality management may find that they have to be recertified in order to take account of the way in which documents are managed in a CMS.

Staff resources and training

The staff skills and expertise required to implement the content management strategy should be considered, including training needs, and the extent to which content-related tasks should be included in job descriptions and evaluations should be addressed. It can be useful to plot content contributors on a grid. See Figure 4.1.

	Good HTML/web skills	Poor HTML/web skills
Good content knowledge		
Poor content knowledge		

Figure 4.1 Table of content contributors

The aim of the grid in Figure 4.2 is to identify training requirements. Staff with poor content knowledge may be support staff in a department who are presented with documents and asked to add them to the system.

Business case

The basis on which a business case for the adoption of a content management system can be made should be set out. This could be based on, for example:

- improved productivity
- speed of adding material to an intranet
- providing audit trails for decisions.

It is important to identify groups of staff that will see early benefits from the adoption of a content management system. At this stage the business plan is in outline only, but it is still worth capturing the key issues. The development of the business case itself is covered in Chapter 6.

Risk analysis

The risks to the organization of implementing a CMS solution must be assessed. They might include:

- resistance to changes in business practice
- disruption to current business
- unforeseen costs

- increased levels of IT support
- no apparent benefits to staff.

Implementation issues

This section should identify some of the possible implementation problems that have arisen from the research. These might be

- heavily over-committed staff in key departments
- lack of management vision
- budgets based on current year only
- lack of technical skills in an IT department.

Glossary

It can be helpful to include a glossary of key terms used in the strategic plan, especially any technical terms that may be unfamiliar to some readers.

Summary

- For both websites and intranets it is important that a content management strategy is developed that meets the needs of both the organization and of users.
- An important component of a content management strategy is the identification of the way in which content flows around the organization.
- The development of a content management strategy requires careful preparation and should be carried out on a collaborative basis.

Reference

Wood, S. (2004) *Information Auditing: a guide for information managers*, Ashford, FreePint Ltd, www.freepint.com.

5 Technology options and costs

Introduction

The processes set out in the previous chapters are designed to identify whether or not an investment in content management software can be justified in principle. Before making the business case consideration must now be given to the range of content management software options that are available, and the costs that will be incurred in implementing these options. Many organizations fail to appreciate that the costs are not just those of the software licence alone. A lot of other factors need to be taken into consideration in order to develop a Total Cost of Implementation (TCI).

The available options are:

Use open-source software to develop a customized solution
Commission a web agency to build a CMS
Build the CMS in-house
Use an outsourced CMS service
Purchase a proprietary CMS product
Purchase a portal application.

The benefits and issues of each of these options are described below.

Use open-source software

Faced with spending a considerable amount of money on commercial software many organizations, especially in the academic and public sector, see considerable financial benefits in using open-source software to build a CMS. At the heart of open-source software is a database and a scripting language. The database is

usually a variant of SQL; among the popular ones are mySQL and
Zope. A scripting language is a form of programming language; it
enables the developer to create applications much more quickly
than using a language such as C++ or Visual Basic. Among the more
popular languages are PHP (often used with mySQL and the basis
of the Midgard CMS), Perl and Python (the basis of the Zope CMS
application).

The software is downloaded over the internet, or sometimes
provided on a CD-ROM or DVD, and so the product can be
evaluated. However, what is being downloaded is a set of software
tools and not a finished product. This is simultaneously the core
strength and weakness of open-source software. There is a growing
range of 'productized' open-source products. A good illustration is
provided by Zope4Intranets which offers (www.zope.com/Products/
Zope4Intranets):

intranet home page
user desktop
WYSIWYG and client-side document editing
calendar management (events, tasks and journals)
forums (threaded message areas)
contact management
search engine
project artefacts management
collaborative workflow
document/asset library
online help
developing and extending
— Zope application server
— page templates
— event subsystem
— schema-based development
end user personalization
system administration
— platform portability
— user authentication
— user authorization
— external system integration.

The current price in mid-2004 for a Zope4Intranets licence for 500 registered users is $9995. Compared with most commercial products this is still low cost, but in relative, not absolute terms.

Benefits of open-source software

One of the major benefits of open-source software is the community of users that supports the products. This is important because usually there is little documentation with open-source products, though there is a growing number of books on open-source products, especially Zope and MySQL. In theory there are perhaps hundreds, if not thousands, of developers of the most popular open-source products, and they can be reached through e-mail groups and other collaborative applications.

However, it is one thing to send out a message and quite another to get a response. Software developers in other organizations are likely to be as busy as your own developers, and a question may either get no response, or many responses each offering a different solution. There is no requirement on the part of any developer to respond to a query, although there is a requirement to share bugs and fixes, and to offer any specific routines back to the community for the benefit of all. Commercial CMS vendors will usually react quickly to address bugs in their software but the release of new functionality is a commercial decision, based on a number of factors.

Another benefit is that the openness of the code means that it is unlikely to vanish, something that may well start to happen to CMS vendors (see Chapter 7) and so there is a significant amount of future-proofing built into open-source products. There is also considerable flexibility to build a CMS that addresses very closely the requirements of the organization.

Disadvantages of open-source software

There is, however, no such thing as a free lunch. With the benefits come some issues that need to be considered very carefully. The first of these is that developers need to be paid a salary, and so even if the software is free there are some development costs, and these can mount up quite quickly. Organizations that have built their IT platforms around Microsoft, IBM and other industry standards may not have the requisite software expertise in-house, and will have to recruit and support developers (or subcontract the development) just for one specific application.

Open-source software products are also mainly run in stand-alone applications. If it is a requirement to link the CMS into an HR system then the integration may be quite difficult, and there is a real risk that the provider of the HR application may not want to share the code required to undertake the integration. For this reason IT directors have an aversion to open-source products because they may have unpredictable impacts on mission-critical systems, and there is no one to sue if the systems go down. However, this situation is changing. One example is the Icoya CMS which is a low-cost product based on Zope for which there is an approved application integration with the SAP enterprise resource planning application.

OSCOM (www.oscom.org) is the International Association for Open Source Content Management. As well as acting as a clearing house for information on open source CMS products OSCOM supports a number of projects related to open-source CMS. These include CMSML, an XML to describe content management frameworks, systems and editors. This project will develop a comprehensive feature list for CMS, a controlled vocabulary to describe these features, and appropriate names for each in XML.

The main message with open-source software is *caveat emptor*. These solutions can be cost effective, but not for all organizations: and choosing this route just to keep inside a budget that was not properly researched in the first place will almost certainly lead to disaster.

Commission a web agency to build a CMS

Many web agencies and software companies have the skills to build a content management system for their clients. Since a CMS is, to a significant extent, a database application, there is a range of options that the agency can use. The larger companies may use Microsoft CM products such as Microsoft Content Server, or build the application using a standard SQL database product from companies such as Oracle or Microsoft. Another option is to build the CMS using open-source software.

Benefits

The web agency will be familiar with the existing website, and will be able to ensure that migration issues (see Chapter 12) are clearly identified.

If the agency has already invested in building a CMS for other clients the cost of adapting the software could be quite low.

Issues

It is likely that the agency will retain the rights to the software. The situation, should the agency close down or be acquired, or the organization decides to use a different agency for web design, need to be assessed carefully.

The software development team may be very small. The loss of one member of this team could be critical to the level of support and development.

The functionality may not be adequate for an intranet, especially in terms of metadata management, workflow and security management, because these features are not often required for a website.

The agency may wish to host the software on its own server.

A web agency designed CMS will not be able to offer document management capability and may have only limited search functionality.

Build the CMS in-house

This is a variant of the option of using a web agency, outlined above.

Benefits

The IT department should be familiar with the existing website, and will be able to ensure that migration issues (see Chapter 12) are clearly identified.

The solution will be tailored around the specific IT platforms that the organization uses, and so application integration should be less of an issue.

The development process should be more transparent.

Unless there is a charge-back from the IT department, development costs will be absorbed within the overheads of the organization.

Issues

The IT department may have to recruit developers with specific expertise which cannot be used for other projects.
The software development team may be very small. The loss of one member of this team could be critical to the level of support and development.
This may well be seen as a 'small' project and may be given a lower priority than other projects.
All development costs will have to be borne by the organization.
A CMS built in-house will not be able to offer document management capability and may have only limited search functionality.

Use an outsourced CMS service

In the early days of intranet deployment in the late 1990s a number of companies entered the market with externally hosted software services. These failed to prove very popular, but more recently there has been renewed interest in this type of solution. For smaller organizations seeking a solution to website content management they are worth investigating. An issue for consideration by European companies using a hosted intranet server is that personal data may be exported to the USA. This may breach EU legislation on data privacy, and any organization contemplating this approach is advised to obtain expert legal advice.

Benefits

Implementation times are short.
This is a cost-effective solution for some web publishing applications.

Issues

Proprietary software makes migration to another system difficult.
Migration of current pages can be difficult.
Support for dynamic databases can be limited.
There is no ability to link to other applications within the
organization.
Data are hosted off-site.

Purchase a proprietary CMS product

Although some commercial CMS products are based on open-
source software this option relates to proprietary CMS products
where the software code remains confidential to the vendor. The
range of products is now vast, with probably around 1000 vendors,
ranging in size from companies operating on a multinational basis
to those providing services on a national market basis. Increasingly
the larger vendors are offering document and records management
applications as well as web content management

Benefits

There has been very considerable investment in software
development stimulated by having to remain competitive on a
cost/functionality basis.
The products are supported by trained professional services staff
with a commitment to customer satisfaction to ensure additional
sales of software and services.
Development costs can be amortized across the entire client base.
Many vendors can provide multi-site, multi-country and multiple
language support.

Issues

Complex feature sets and pricing models make it very difficult to
compare products.
There is limited ability for customers to carry out customization.
The vendor may go out of business or be acquired.
There can be substantial consulting costs in addition to the
software licence.

Purchase a portal application

There is currently considerable interest in implementing portal applications, especially in the academic and corporate sectors. Portal applications provide two important features for users:

They integrate a wide range of different applications onto the PC desktop.
Usually a user can personalize this desktop so that only specific applications are presented.

In general a portal application does not provide the means to add content to the portal, such as a content management system. Although this is gradually changing in the near term implementing a portal application will not provide a solution to content management requirements.

Total Cost of Implementation

The cost of the software license is usually only the tip of the iceberg when it comes to working out the Total Cost of Implementation to feed into the business case. This is especially the case with proprietary CMS products. The high-end products are much more a set of tools than an out-of-the-box solution, and considerable effort will be required to customize the CMS for a specific organization. The scale of the costs can be at least as much again as the core software licence, and could be up to four times as much for high-end products in complex web environments. See Table 5.1.

Table 5.1 CMS cost elements

Cost element	Comment
Initial work to develop a business case, statement of requirements and support for vendor selection	This can be carried out by the organization, but may need to be subcontracted to consultants.
CMS base licence cost	A range of licensing models can make this difficult to estimate at the outset.
Database application licence cost	There may be a need to purchase an additional licence for an SQL database.

(*Continued on next page*)

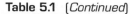

Table 5.1 (*Continued*)

Cost element	Comment
Annual support fee	This is typically 20% of the CMS base licence cost, and often starts from the date the software is purchased.
CMS hardware	There may be a need to purchase additional server and other hardware, and upgrade the desktop environment.
Search software costs	A range of licensing models can make this difficult to estimate at the outset.
Cost of scoping study to produce final quotation	This may be bundled in to the licence cost but is often billed separately. The cost varies with the vendor.
Implementation costs	These are the costs of using external consultants to customize the product to the specific requirements of the customer.
Training costs	These costs depend on whether training is carried out on site or on the vendor's premises.
Content migration costs	The volume of work may be such that this has to be contracted out.

Search and classification software

There are two different search requirements within a CMS:

The first is for authors to be able to search through the content in the CMS repository so that previous versions of the content, or a related piece of content, can be found to act as the basis for new content.

The second is to enable users to search through the website or intranet for content.

The first requirement is often met by the vendor integrating one of the enterprise search engines, such as those offered by Verity and Convera, but often only in a stripped-down 'light' version tailored for the special CMS application. This application will usually only run on the CMS pre-production server, not on the published sites.

An additional complication is that the search features for a website are not adequate for an intranet site, for example:

There may be no requirement to search the content of pdf files on the website, only the metadata attached to them. In an intranet there will almost certainly be a need to provide pdf content searching.

Relevance ranking may need to be carried out in a different way, and intranet applications are likely to benefit from being able to customize the way that search hits are displayed.

Document security is also an issue. On a website, by definition, everything is publicly available. On an intranet it is important for a user to carry out a search only on those documents that they are entitled to see.

In some organizations there may be a number of intranets, not all of which are using the same CMS, if indeed they are using a CMS at all. There will be a requirement to search across all the intranet servers, and this is unlikely to be possible with a search engine that is adapted specifically to identify content for authors.

The end result is that to the cost of implementing a CMS there needs to be added the cost of implementing a search engine. Even if the decision is made to implement the search engine at a later stage, perhaps once the CMS itself is operational, planning for the search implementation needs to be started at the outset so that a realistic figure for the Total Cost of Implementation can be determined over (say) a three-year period.

Matching costs to budgets

Faced with the mounting costs of implementing a CMS many organizations look for ways to reduce costs to keep within a budget that was probably allocated on either an arbitrary basis or on the basis of a discussion at an exhibition stand with a single vendor. There are some options open to an organization to reduce the Total Cost of Implementation, but all come with an element of risk attached. See Table 5.2.

Table 5.2 Options and risks in Total Cost of Implementation

Cost element	Options and risks
Initial work to develop a business case, statement of requirements and support for vendor selection	This can be undertaken internally, saving the cost of consultants, but is there enough staff expertise available, and can the organization afford to allocate such staff to this work?
CMS base licence cost	Open-source software can substantially reduce this cost, but the development costs can be high, and there must be a more rigorous internal project management process which will add to costs, even if indirectly.
Database application licence cost	This may not be required, depending on the current licence agreement.
Annual support fee	For commercial software this cannot be reduced.
CMS hardware	This is not a substantial element of the Total Cost of Implementation.
Search software costs	A low-cost/open-source solution can be implemented, but the benefits of using a CMS may then be negated.
Cost of scoping study to produce final quotation	This is not required if an open-source solution is being used.
Implementation costs	With commercial products there is usually only a very limited amount of work that can be carried out by in-house IT and web staff.
Training costs	It may be possible to reduce these costs through negotiation.
Content migration costs	There is a very substantial amount of work involved, and if the web team carries this out then time to develop the site using the CMS will be very limited.

Summary

Purchasing a commercial CMS product is not the only option, just one of many, each with benefits and challenges.

Open-source software will certainly mean that there is no licence cost, but the development effort involved may mean that the Total Cost of Implementation is not significantly different to other options.

The cost of implementing a commercial CMS will certainly be more than the licence costs by a factor of 2–4 times.

Few CMS products have full search functionality for users of the site.

6 Making the business case

Introduction

Most organizations require some form of business case to justify the investment in a CMS application. The fundamental problem is that there is unlikely to be any quantification of the costs of maintaining the current website or intranet site, so any financial case is very difficult to make. The problems are further compounded because few, if any, of the senior managers involved in the business case review will have any prior knowledge of content management; and few (regrettably!) will be aware of the work involved in managing the web assets of the organization.

When the management team reviews a business case for a finance package or an HR package it is usually the case that there is already a system in place and so, to a large extent, it is a question of replacing like for like. In addition the core sponsor, such as the Finance Director or the HR Director, is sitting at the table, and there is a general view that they know what they want, and that if it doesn't work their reputation is on the line. A CMS may be replacing almost no system at all, and the sponsor may be, by default, any of the managers involved in the budget review process, but may have no personal commitment to the success of the project. Cynically, but all too often, the situation is that if the CMS is a success then the sponsor will wish to be seen as a hero, but if not then it was not really their direct responsibility in any case, and they walk away from it.

An effective business plan for a CMS therefore has to be an adroit mixture of vision and reality, and that is quite a challenge.

At this stage of the *Handbook* it might be useful to see where we are in the process. Chapter 2 set out at a detailed level what a CMS does, and Chapter 3 introduced the concepts of information architecture and metadata which are essential in achieving a successful CMS implementation. There will now be a good view of the content assets of the organization as a result of the information and content audits suggested in Chapter 4, and the technology options described in Chapter 5 have probably been reduced to one or two. But so far no decisions have been made that cannot be reversed. With the preparation of the business plan the CMS project starts to have considerable visibility, and if a good plan is prepared and then adopted the chances are that the expectations of many will have been raised to the point that it is not so much a question of 'if' but 'when'.

'When', along with 'How much' are two very difficult questions to answer with a CMS implementation, and there is a danger in being too explicit on both counts.

The fundamental issues with a CMS business case include the following:

- It is very difficult to make a business case based on a quantifiable return-on-investment calculation. If the only way your organization assesses projects is on this basis it may be that a business case cannot be made.
- The business case for implementing a CMS for a website is somewhat different from the business case for an intranet. A website business case can make some assumptions about increases in levels of use and revenue, whereas an intranet business case is often about supporting knowledge management or providing better access to information.
- The investment for a CMS will almost certainly go over the current budget year, and this can be a major issue for many organizations, especially in the public and not-for-profit sectors.
- The business case must usually be made at an organizational level, and not just the departmental level that would be applicable for a library management application.
- Especially in the intranet environment the business processes themselves must be changed, and the implications of these changes and the optimum timing are not easy to forecast at the outset.
- CMS is not a technology per se, but a means of enabling people to accomplish organizational objectives. If the organizational objectives are not clear, then the benefits of implementing a CMS will fail to materialize.

What problems could a CMS solve?

It was tempting to start this section with the sub-title 'What problems *will* a CMS solve?' but if it is not the right CMS implemented in the right way then the problems will not be solved.

Table 6.1 sets out some of the problems that organizations face in managing content, which may be helpful in deciding whether or not a CMS is going to make any significant impact on the organization. The table is as valid for a website as an intranet.

Table 6.1 Content management problems

Current Problem	Score 3 = essential to solve 2 = useful to solve 1 = no significant benefit
There is lack of consistency between the pages that makes it difficult to browse around the site.	
It is difficult to make global changes to the site to reflect new branding, a new range of products or a new department.	
Every web author has to be trained on FrontPage or Dreamweaver.	
When someone leaves it is very difficult to identify which pages they were responsible for.	
Managing links takes a lot of time.	
Content publishing is hindered by the need to go through a web master.	
It is important to be able to roll back the site for regulatory/compliance/audit reasons.	
There is no way of identifying information that is out of date.	
There are often multiple versions of the same document on the site.	
There is a need to generate HTML and pdf formats from the original file.	
It is difficult to manage graphics and other specialist file formats that add value to the site.	
When staff are away it would be useful for them to be able to define a date so that content they have authored will be published when they are out of the office.	
The organization is changing rapidly and it is difficult to make changes to the sites on a timely basis.	

(Continued on next page)

Table 6.1 (*Continued*)

Current Problem	Score 3 = essential to solve 2 = useful to solve 1 = no significant benefit
It is very difficult to introduce levels of security to access content at either a document collection or a specific document level.	
The search engine is not effective because of inadequate or inconsistent metadata.	
We would like to give different user groups their own customized view of the site but the effort involved is too great.	
We have some databases that it would be valuable to provide users with access to through the site.	

If you scored honestly and your total is more than 30 then the chances are that a CMS will be able to solve your problems, but only if there is a commitment on the part of the organization to work in different ways in order to make the best use of the features available. If your score is less than 15 then buying this *Handbook* has probably saved you a lot of money and a great deal of effort.

Linking the business plan to organizational objectives

The business case for a CMS has to be linked as directly as possible to organizational objectives, and must not be made only on the basis of productivity gains. The main reason for this is that it is very difficult to quantify productivity gains because few organizations have any ideas about how much it costs to prepare a document or to add content to the website. The exception may be in professional services firms that charge on an hourly basis, but probably not for staff that would be involved directly in maintaining a website or intranet.

In many organizations there is no formal information management strategy (or if there is it turns out to be an IT strategy, which is not the same) and so the information management strategy needs to be developed along with the content management strategy. The steps in the process are outlined in the shaded panel opposite.

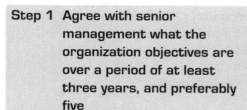

Step 1 Agree with senior management what the organization objectives are over a period of at least three years, and preferably five

These objectives could be along the lines of:

- Continue to expand our product range.
- Improve the margins on our core businesses.
- Acquire some niche companies to expand our business interests.
- Develop our business interests in China.
- Aim to be No. 3 in market share by 2006.

Step 2 Extend these objectives into information requirements

- Continue to expand our product range:
  - more content to be available on the site
  - might need to have a more flexible information architecture
  - new departments may be set up
  - may be a need to expand our taxonomy.
- Improve the margins on our core businesses:
  - better range of information on the intranet
  - more forms and self-service applications

  - improve the access to management information
  - support communities of practice to capitalize on knowledge.
- Acquire some niche companies to expand our business interests:
  - need to set up intranet pages that provide an introduction to the organization
  - may have to integrate other content management applications
  - could be a requirement to change the document security model.
- Develop our business interests in China:
  - may have to manage third-party translation of content
  - CMS would have to support Chinese character sets
  - assess the browser environment in China.
- Aim to be No.3 in market share by 2006:
  - need to benchmark competitor sites and be ready to respond with innovations
  - increased requirement for e-business applications
  - assess server capacity.

Step 3 Develop a content management strategy

The model for the content management strategy itself is set out in Chapter 1. See also Figure 6.1 overleaf.

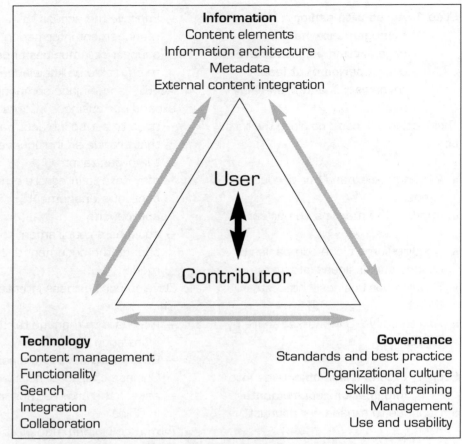

Information
Content elements
Information architecture
Metadata
External content integration

User

Contributor

Technology
Content management
Functionality
Search
Integration
Collaboration

Governance
Standards and best practice
Organizational culture
Skills and training
Management
Use and usability

Figure 6.1 The elements of a content management strategy

Benefits of linking content management and business strategies

There are some important benefits in linking the content management strategy to the business strategy:

- There is visibility and buy-in to the project from senior staff.
- Resource allocation can be set against direct impacts on the achievement of these objectives.
- If the link with planning departments and senior managers is maintained, as it should be, changes in objectives will be picked up and incorporated into the next version of the content strategy.
- Content authoring is more likely to be seen as being a defined element in job descriptions.
- The CMS implementation is seen as an enterprise-level project.

- The implications for integration with other applications can be assessed.
- The overall benefits and risks of the project are easier to assimilate.

The not-for-profit sector

The point is sometimes made that using a revenue perspective is only possible with the for-profit sector, and that organizations in the not-for-profit sector are in a more difficult position. However, even a not-for-profit organization must have income from somewhere. An illustration might be a UK university, which has the following sources of revenue:

- government funding of undergraduate students from the UK
- fee payments of undergraduate students from the EU and other countries
- government funding and fee payments of postgraduate students from the UK
- fee payments of postgraduate students from the EU and other countries
- research sponsorship
- contract research
- exploitation of research results through patents and licence income
- establishment of business ventures
- sales of reports, books and other items
- gifts and bequests
- conferences and other events.

All of these can be supported by an effective website, and this analysis takes no account of the internal, campus-user requirements which might be met from an intranet/portal or campus-level website.

Creating a vision

Many organizations find that people at all levels do not have a vision of how a CMS would work on a day-to-day basis. It is often the case that senior managers without technical knowledge fail to realize the challenges of managing large websites with a product such as FrontPage; if that is the case the blame lies not just with their level of understanding but also with the web team for not getting the message across.

There are two aspects of vision creation that need to be addressed in the development of a business case that sells the need for a CMS. The first is external vision of how the website or intranet would be more responsive to changes in user requirements, and that can be achieved through the development of the personas and scenarios described in Chapter 3.

In addition there needs to be a vision of how the internal processes will change as a result of the introduction of a CMS. There are two possible approaches:

- Take a recent major site change, perhaps the addition of a new section or a global change relating to a company that had just been acquired, and show the steps involved and the time taken to undertake this work. Alongside this analysis set out for comparison the way the same process would have been accomplished using a CMS. One effective example is often site roll-back, because this is complex with a conventional site but quite straightforward with a CMS. This facility is of value to both a website and an intranet.
- Purchase an inexpensive CMS product, perhaps based on an open-source product, and demonstrate how a CMS works in practice. Although of course there is an investment in the time to learn the software, the benefits can be substantial, not only in terms of creating a vision of CMS operations but also for the project team to learn more about the functionality of a CMS. A good example of such a product would be Bricolage (http://bricolage.cc/) which has some good screen shots on the site which show the key steps in using a content management application. Indeed the Bricolage site sets a level of communication about CMS applications which is considerably higher than that of most commercial vendors.

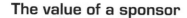

The value of a sponsor

The impact of the CMS implementation will be enterprise wide, or global for a website. There needs to be a significant level of understanding and commitment from the most senior levels of the organization, something that is not likely to be an issue with a new HR or finance system. A CMS is a substantial undertaking for an organization and the support of a senior member of staff as a sponsor is essential. One of the important roles for the sponsor is to ensure that any cross-departmental issues are dealt with in a fair and open way. The level of the sponsorship will also indicate to the organization the value that is being placed on the implementation.

Planning for the future

Implementing a CMS is a long-term commitment. Apart from any other consideration it may well take a year from the initial decision to explore the benefits to the time when the system is fully operational. This may mean that the cost of the system has to be taken out of the budgets in two successive years, a substantial problem for organizations that can spend only on a year-on-year basis.

Any business plan for a CMS has to take as a minimum a two-year view of the future, and ideally a three-year view, even if Year 3 is only pencilled in at the present time.

Some of the issues to be considered include:

- Will the organization be replacing or investing in IT systems that interface with the CMS, such as an HR portal? The choice of CMS may limit the organization in the selection of a new portal.
- Will new regulatory requirements impact on the way the organization manages information? An example in the UK would be the way in which the legal system is moving towards electronic document management in civil and criminal cases.
- Are there plans to move the organization into new business areas? This may affect the taxonomy and metadata schemes that have been devised.
- Will the workforce increasingly work on a remote basis? This may have implications for the bandwidth available for access to an intranet.

- Is the organization likely to acquire, or merge with, another organization, and if so is the CMS platform extensible and scalable? Of course mergers and acquisitions are always difficult to predict, but some companies make public statements of their ambitions in this direction.
- Will senior staff be retiring in the near future? This may lead to new staff coming into the organization with different priorities and ambitions.

Since the future is still very uncertain the best that can be achieved may be the development of some scenarios that at least enable the risks and benefits of a specific CMS strategy to be evaluated on a formal basis.

There are examples where organizations have replaced one web CMS with another, but the cost of conversion is high even in a web environment. Taking out a fully featured CMS that is dealing with web content and document management is a process full of uncertainty and risk, especially if there is major disruption to business processes.

Summary

- An effective business plan for a CMS has to be an adroit mixture of vision and reality.
- It is unrealistic to try to make the business case on a numeric 'return-on-investment' basis because few organizations can put a figure on the current cost of content management.
- The business plan should be linked to the corporate plan and to those objectives of the organization that are information-critical.
- A senior-level sponsor for the business plan is highly desirable because the impact of implementing a CMS will have an impact on every visitor to the website and/or every employee using the intranet.

7 The CMS business

Introduction

The CMS business is not yet ten years old. Only quite recently have there been the first moves in industry consolidation that are feature of any maturing industry sector. Virtually all the largest companies are US-owned, and some (such as Percussion) remain privately owned. These have to disclose comparatively little financial information about their operations. In selecting a CMS vendor it can be very useful to understand the antecedents of the company because they give an indication of the strengths of the product and the likely development routes.

Vendor–client relationships

For companies offering only CMS products there are two sources of revenue. The first is from the sales of the product itself and the second is from the provision of consulting services to support the implementation of the product. These latter services are often referred to as 'professional services'. Not all CMS vendors offer professional services, either because their product is designed to be implemented by the customer out of the box, or because they work with systems integration companies who provide professional service support on behalf of the CMS vendor.

A common approach is for the CMS vendor to provide professional service support in strategically important market sectors, such as finance, manufacturing, retail and pharmaceutical companies. These are substantial market sectors and there are benefits to the CMS vendor in building up expertise in the work processes of these companies because there is a very good chance that this expertise can be used in other companies. For smaller sectors, such as charities or the education market, it will usually make better commercial sense to work with partner companies who already sell IT and software services to these sectors, using the expertise of the partner to support the implementation process.

Although this makes good financial sense a common problem is that the consulting skills needed to manage content/information projects are in scarce supply in many systems integration companies, and moreover these companies do not do enough work to remain familiar with the features of the latest version of the CMS software. There have been instances in the UK where the partner has conducted the implementation of a CMS without any reference to the CMS vendor, who then has to spend some considerable time and effort in remedial work when the partner has failed to understand either the requirements or the software. Such situations are the exception rather than the rule, but the possibility of problems occurring does need to be included in the risk log referred to in Chapter 8.

Table 7.1 is a list of CMS vendors. In view of the fact that there are around 700 vendors of CMS products worldwide the list is inevitably selective. A list of sites that attempt to catalogue CMS products is given in Chapter 13.

The web content management industry

The initial catalyst for the web content management industry was the need for companies to manage large complex websites in the early days of the dot.com business in 1998–2001. An important feature of these sites was the provision of e-business and e-commerce applications. Among the current vendors who can trace their business origins to this period are Broadvision, Interwoven, Stellent and Vignette in the USA and Mediasurface in the UK. At the time these companies were established XML was still in its infancy and over the last two to three years these companies have had to substantially enhance their products to support XML.

In terms of the leading IT companies, such as IBM and Microsoft, the CMS vendors are quite small companies. To take Vignette as an example, the company has around 800 employees and total revenues for the fourth quarter of 2003 were $39.2 million with licence revenue representing $16.2 million of total revenue.

Table 7.1 A selective list of CMS vendors

Activedition	Dundee, Scotland	www.activedition.com
Atomz	San Francisco, USA	www.atomz.com
Bricolage	San Francisco, USA	www.bricolage.cc
Contensis	London, UK	www.contensis.co.uk
Crown Peak	Los Angeles, USA	www.crownpeak.com
Day	Basel, Switzerland	www.day.com
Documentum	Pleasanton, USA	www.documentum.com
Ektron	Amherst, USA	www.ektron.com
Fatwire	New York, USA	www.fatwire.com
FileNet	Costa Mesa, USA	www.filenet.com
Goss Interactive	Plymouth, UK	www.gossinteractive.com
Hummingbird	Toronto, Canada	www.hummingbird.com
Hyperwave	Munich, Germany	www.hyperwave.com
Icoya	Frankfurt, Germany	www.icoya.com
Immediacy	Poole, UK	www.immediacy.co.uk
Ingeniux	Seattle, USA	www.ingeniux.com
Interwoven	Sunnyvale, USA	www.interwoven.com
Libertas	Armagh, Northern Ireland	www.libertas-solutions.com
Mediasurface	Newbury, UK	www.mediasurface.com
Microsoft	Seattle, USA	www.microsoft.com
Objective	Sydney, Australia	www.objective.com
Open Text	Waterloo, Canada	www.opentext.com
PaperThin	Quincy, USA	www.paperthin.com
Percussion	Stoneham, USA	www.percussion.com
Polopoly	Stockholm, Sweden	www.polopoly.com
RedDot	Oldenburg, Germany	www.reddot.com
Roxen	Linköping, Sweden	www.roxen.com
Solid8	London, UK	www.solid8.com
Stellent	Minneapolis, USA	www.stellent.com
Terminal Four	Dublin, Eire	www.termimalfour.com
Tridion	Amsterdam, Netherlands	www.tridion.com
Vignette	Austin, USA	www.vignette.com
VYRE	London, UK	www.vyre.com
Xpansys	Middlesborough, UK	www.xpansys.com

For the year ending 31 December 2003, total revenue was $158.3 million, with licence revenue representing $61 million of total revenue. These figures illustrate the business model mentioned above, with software licence revenues accounting for less than 50% of total revenue. However, these licence revenues are not just sales to new customers but include ongoing income from the (usually) 20% annual maintenance fees that are charged to customers.

As a further example, Stellent revenues for the quarter ending 31 March 2004 were $20.6 million. Revenues for the fiscal year ending 31 March 2004 were $75.8 million, a 16% increase over revenues of $65.4 million in the previous year. Licence revenues represented 55%, and service revenues 45%, of the total revenue for the quarter ending 31 March 2004.

Privately-owned companies generally publish very little financial information. In the case of Percussion a press release dated 17 February 2004 explained:

> Demand for its content management software products rose significantly, driving a 30 percent increase in sales over the first half of 2003. In addition, boosted by growing momentum in European sales, the company also posted record-high Q4 results across all product lines.

Defining whether or not these and other CMS vendors are currently profitable is not easy because US accounting rules offer a number of different approaches to defining 'profitability' for software companies. At the present time the profitability of CMS vendors is marginal at best because they invest in product development and use their share capital to acquire niche software and services companies to broaden the feature range they are able to offer customers. A useful indicator of a successful company is the growth in sales of software to new customers, and this can often be difficult to determine. The ongoing challenge for a CM vendor is the cost of product development, especially because this has to be undertaken in a way that maintains the integrity of older versions of the software.

The need for financial due diligence

The financial situation of these companies presents a potential customer with two issues:

- Will the company be in business for the likely lifespan of the CMS software, which should be at least three years, and preferably five?
- Many organizations require contractors to provide, for example, three years of financial information and are keen to see that there is a record of financial stability and, preferably, profitability. For UK customers the problem is made worse by the fact that there is usually no UK financial information that can be disclosed. When the organization is buying a new product from a US IT industry leader, such as Oracle or HP, then the sheer size of the company is a comfort. Other products brought from US vendors are usually low-cost hardware and software products where the financial situation of the company is not of any real significance. CMS applications, which may range in licence cost from $30,000 upwards, present some difficult issues for the finance department in the organization, especially in the public sector.

Given the still small size of the market it is surprising that very few companies have gone out of business. Reef was a Belgian CMS vendor that ran out of funding and divine was a US conglomerate that acquired a number of software companies (and the RoweCom subscription agency) before going bankrupt. In the case of divine both the CMS products, Open Market and ePrise, were acquired by other companies and continue in use.

Of course not all CMS vendors are US-owned. It is difficult to even estimate the number of CMS products on the market, but world-wide the number is probably in excess of 700. Many of these are companies that have a strong national market in Europe and over the last couple of years have started to expand into other European markets, or even the USA. Examples include Objective (Australia), Tridion (the Netherlands), Mediasurface (UK), Roxen (Sweden) and RedDot (Germany). Local support for multi-site/multiple language/multinational companies is an important consideration for many organizations, and the level of support varies considerably from company to company. Even where a company appears to have an office it may be only a sales agency and not a full-service office with consulting support. For the larger US-owned CMS vendors all the research and development is carried out in the USA, and even though there is often very good local support there may still be a requirement to deal with the development teams in the USA, and these may well be in California, making real-time contact during the European working day somewhat difficult.

The document management industry

The document management industry is somewhat older than the web content management industry. FileNet was founded in 1982 and Documentum in 1990. These companies, and others like them such as Open Text and Xerox, developed the business of managing large complex documents (such as aircraft manuals) and large volumes of scanned documents such as letters and forms for the insurance and other sectors. Over the last couple of years these companies have started to develop web content management applications so that they can up-sell to their existing customers, and offer a complete document life-cycle management solution to new customers. The web functionality has often been developed through the acquisition of small specialist companies, such as the acquisition by Documentum of eRoom (to provide collaboration services for intranet applications) and Bulldog (to provide digital asset management features).

The portal and applications integration industry

In the late 1990s there was very considerable enthusiasm for what were often referred to as Enterprise Information Portals (EIP) which integrated a range of applications (usually web-based) onto a customizable desktop. For reasons that need not be considered here most of the venture-capital based portal vendors failed to make it through the dot.com crash, among the exceptions being Plumtree (still an independent vendor) and Epicentric (purchased in 2003 by Vignette).

The content management capability of portal software was usually non-existent, and it is only quite recently that the portal vendors (and that includes the Microsoft SharePoint portal application) have begun to strengthen this aspect of their product range.

A number of companies offer application integration at a somewhat higher level of functionality than at the desktop, for example BEA and ATG. As with portal software their content management capabilities are much more limited at present than a high-end CMS product, but this may change in the future.

Summary

- The CMS industry is still in the process of maturing, though little consolidation is taking place.
- The larger vendors are acquiring niche businesses in order to offer integrated enterprise-level solutions.
- There may well be over 1000 CMS products on the market, although only perhaps 50 have a sizeable client base.
- For many companies revenues from the provision of consulting services to support implementation are a significant source of revenue.

8 Managing the project

Introduction

The implementation of a CMS is a very complex process. It is very important that it is treated as a formal project, and not just as something that the web team can cope with on top of all its other activities. Many organizations make the mistake of appointing the web manager as the project manager. Project management is a discipline in its own right, requiring an adroit blend of attention to detail, the ability to take decisions on trade-offs between different options, and first-class people management and communication skills. Even if the web manager has these skills in addition to technical and design knowledge the organization has to consider whether they can in fact be spared to run the project.

Managing a CMS implementation is a full-time project, certainly from the point at which work commences on a statement of requirements right up to the full release of the new site. This could well take nine to twelve months, and during that time the chances that a web manager will be able to spent an adequate amount of time on both the project and ongoing web management activities are remote.

CMS project elements

The main elements of a CMS project implementation are listed in the shaded panel. Not included in this analysis is the work required to design a new information architecture, design and implement new page layouts, develop metadata schemes and perhaps change business processes to take advantage of the CMS. Also excluded is the selection and purchase of search software. Table 8.1 (page 90) gives a summary of the process.

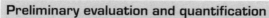

Preliminary evaluation and quantification

The initial stage of work to assess the extent to which implementing a CMS is a realistic and appropriate course of action could extend over several months, if not longer. As discussed in Chapter 6 a significant amount of quantification of the scale of the problem needs to be carried out before a business case can be developed. This period of time varies so much between organizations that setting a typical duration for this work is not helpful. For the purposes of setting out a basic timeline for the project this analysis starts with the preparation of a business case.

Making the business case   1–3 months

This has been covered in Chapter 6. As far as the project schedule is concerned the case can take some time to review, and the funds and other resources requested may not be readily available, so a significantly longer period of time may be necessary.

Writing the statement of requirements (SoR)   1–2 months

This document can have a variety of titles, others being Invitation to Tender and Request for a Proposal. As is set out in Chapter 9 this needs to be a detailed and well considered document because it will determine to a very significant extent the overall success of the project. Writing the initial draft may well take a month overall, and it is essential that this is then circulated to all the stakeholders for comment and revision.

Vendor response   1–2 months

The speed with which a CMS vendor can respond to the SoR depends very much on the clarity of the SoR and the ease with which the vendor can adapt existing text to complete a proposal. In the UK, CMS vendors have quite small staff numbers. Writing a response to an SoR takes not only technical knowledge but also commercial expertise. The response will form the basis for a contract in due course, so there could be quite a high level of sign-off from within the CMS vendor, and this all takes time to accomplish. In the public sector in most countries there are rigorous procurement regulations. In the EU the tender may have to be published in the Official Journal of the EU, and this requires a 52-day period for a response to the SoR.

(Continued on next page)

(*Continued*)

Initial proposal review   **1 month**

The responses may vary widely in size and complexity. Even if quite tight rules
have been set for the presentation of the proposal there may be quite a wide
variation in the structure and content of the proposals. This means that just
looking through the proposals to find the prices being quoted is not an adequate
basis for selection. In any case it is very unusual for a proposal to contain a fixed-
price quotation for the implementation.

Vendor presentations   **1 month**

Even if visits have been made to some, or all, of the vendors who have submitted
proposals it is essential for a formal presentation to take place which covers
specific issues raised in the statement of requirements. Because of the number
of people involved (see Chapter 10) setting up these meetings at short notice can
be very difficult to achieve.

Vendor selection   **1–2 months**

From the proposals and the presentations it should be possible to select a
preferred vendor and an alternate vendor. A considerable amount of information
will now have been gained, but more needs to be added from visits to reference
sites. These may take some time to arrange becuse dates have to be agreed with
the reference site, the vendor's sales team and the organization's project team.
Even if the visit lasts only a few hours it could take several days to set it up.

Scoping study   **1 month**

The proposal from the CMS vendor will usually be indicative, and dependent on
the vendor gaining a substantial amount of knowledge. As a first step the vendor
will undertake a scoping study. This will look in more detail at the requirements,
especially any potentially tricky ones that arise during the presentations; it will
consider the IT and network environment, and also the way in which the current
website pages are stored to assess any migration issues. Once this has been
completed the vendor may be willing to provide a fixed-price quotation, but even
then there may be some areas, usually migration of legacy data, where the
proposal will be worded with some care: it is not until migration starts that the
full scale of any problems starts to emerge.

(*Continued on next page*)

(Continued)

Contract negotiation   **1 month**

The process of contract negotiation can take several weeks. Some CMS vendors are privately-owned companies in the USA. This can give rise to problems in some organizations that undertake an acceptable level of due diligence in assessing the financial stability of the vendor.

Implementation   **2–6 months**

The length of time for this part of the project is the most difficult to forecast. Much will depend on the extent of changes to the information architecture of the site, how well developed the metadata and security models are, and the quality of the file/page management of the original site. Many vendors do have a 'quick start' package, but this may implement only part of the site, or be very dependent on there being a 'clean' site to migrate.

Table 8.1 Summary of CMS implementation timescales

Activity	Range (months)	Best Case	Typical Case
Making the business case	1–3	1	3
Writing the statement of requirements	1–2	2	5
Vendor response	1	3	6
Initial proposal review	1–2	4	8
Vendor presentations	1	5	9
Vendor selection	1–2	6	11
Scoping study	1	7	12
Contract negotiation	1	8	13
Implementation	2–6	10	19

Implications of the procurement schedule

The complexity and duration of CMS implementation give rise to a number of issues which need to be considered in some detail:

- **Change of personnel in the project team** – Care needs to be taken to anticipate the impact of project team staff being appointed to other positions, or leaving the company. It may not always be appropriate to appoint the person taking up the position that was held by a member of the team. It is important to replace the skills and knowledge that the team member contributed to the team, and not just make up the numbers.

MANAGING THE PROJECT ■■■■■

- **Change of project sponsor** – A CMS project needs a sponsor at a senior management level. The consequences of a change of sponsor are highly dependent on when the change takes place.
- **Budget set out over two financial years** – In many organizations, especially in the public and not-for-profit sector, this may require a commitment of budget funds that it is not possible to make. The danger of proceeding with the initial implementation without knowing for certain that funds will be available is that the CMS will never become fully implemented across the organization.
- **Requirements may change** – As a result of business expansion, and acquisition or merger activity, the requirements for the CMS may change. An example may be that initially only the website was to be supported by a CMS, but now a decision has been made to use the CMS for the intranet as well. This will almost certainly change the functionality requirements and the Total Cost of Implementation.

Project management

It should now be clear that the CMS implementation needs to be handled as a formal project, and not just as something that can be managed as part of the ongoing development of the website or intranet. Project management involves more than creating a project plan in Microsoft Project.

Project management problems

Some of the particular problems that will be faced in managing the project include:

- no previous experience on which to base the time it will take to undertake almost any of the tasks associated with the specification, procurement and implementation, even down to how long it will take to gain approval for the budget
- lack of a formal project management framework within the organization
- no project management experience within the web/intranet team
- lack of awareness of the interrelationships between the various elements of the implementation process

91

- heavy reliance on external organizations willing to commit to internal project deadlines, such as contract negotiation
- the project management system used by the selected CMS vendor does not easily integrate with the system being used by the organization.

The problems are difficult enough when there is just the organization and the CMS vendor involved, but if a systems integrator is actually undertaking the CMS implementation on behalf of the vendor, and search/classification software is being implemented at the same time, then the project becomes even more complex to manage.

Many organizations have a formal project management methodology. In the UK most public sector organizations use Prince2 as their project methodology. Many vendors also have their own proprietary project management methodology, and care must be taken to ensure that if there are two different methodologies they do meet in the middle.

Project management success factors

Some of the key success factors in project management, with particular reference to a CMS implementation, are:

- The overall project should be divided into individual work packages, such as the content audit, information architecture, metadata development and the development of a vendor short list.
- Each work package should have a project manager who is responsible for ensuring that the project meets its objectives on time, with the designated resources and to acceptable levels of quality.
- Once the initial work packages have been agreed on a stand-alone basis the extent to which the outcomes of any one package impacts on others should be assessed. This will lead to the development of a critical path through the packages.
- Reporting to the project board needs to be at a level appropriate to the scale and risk of the project, and in general should be exception reporting.

- The terms of reference for the overall project manager and for any managers of individual projects need to be set out clearly so that the people concerned know what decisions can be made without reference to the project board.
- There should be an independent assessment of the quality of any deliverable.
- There should be a well defined process for identifying 'red flag' issues and for agreeing appropriate action.

The use of the term 'red flag' requires some explanation. There is a convention in major projects that a colour code is used so that a set of projects can be visually reviewed for conformance to the project plan. For acceptable conformation the colour green is used; where there is some concern about progress and outcomes the colour yellow is used. A red flag is used when the project is in immediate danger of failing to meet objectives; an agreed set of processes is put in place, such as an immediate meeting of the project board, to ensure that the problem is fully understood and remedial action taken.

Risk management

A key issue in CM implementation is managing the risk of the project. There will be little or no previous experience in the organization about such an implementation and so the risks might not only be high but not even recognized. Taking a proactive approach to risk management is therefore essential.

Risks can be categorized in two ways.

Probability

The first of these is the probability of the risk occurring. An example might include the loss of key personnel within the organization:

- high: 70–100% certain to occur
- medium: 40–69% certain to occur
- low: 0–39% certain to occur.

Impact

The second category is the severity of the impact of the risk:

- high: unable to meet project objectives or major deliverable(s)
- medium: unable to meet a project deliverable, some benefits not achievable
- low: Unable to meet some aspects of requirements, minor scope change.

Risk log

At the outset all the likely risks to the implementation should be set out, even if the probability and/or impact seems to be low. Each risk should then have an action associated with it that seems to be, at that time, the appropriate way to counter the risk.

These typically include:

- **Prevention** – How could the risk be removed?
- **Reduction** – What actions could be taken to reduce either the severity or the impact?
- **Transference** – Could the risk be reduced by transferring it, for example using an external contractor to take the place of a member of staff?
- **Contingency** – There is no immediate way of reducing the risk for certain, but some outline plans are agreed.
- **Acceptance**– Accept the risk, but continue to monitor the situation.

There are other ways to manage risk logs, and in the end it does not matter which is selected so long as it is used on a considered basis.

Summary

- The implementation of a CMS is a complex process and it is very important that it is treated as a formal project, and not just as something that the web team can cope with alongside all its other activities.
- The period from the development of the initial business plan to the full implementation (especially for an intranet) may well be nine to twelve months.
- A formal risk management procedure is essential.

9

Writing a statement of requirements

Introduction

The statement of requirements (SoR) is a document that enables the organization to evaluate proposals from CMS vendors (and of course open-source options) and leads to the signing of a contract and the implementation of the CMS. Organizations have a range of terms for such a document, including an invitation to tender (ITT), and a request for a proposal (RFP). The very fact that it will form the basis of a contract means that the document must be scrutinized by the purchasing and/or legal departments in the organization. They will wish to contribute to the document to ensure that procurement procedures are complied with. Indeed the structure of the document itself may be governed by these procedures.

The objectives of the SoR

All too often these documents are no more than a list of desired functionalities for the CMS that have been derived from various publications, or white papers on CMS vendor websites. Although it is important to understand the functionalities of CMS products, just listing them and asking a vendor to tick the relevant boxes is a totally ineffectual way of selecting a vendor. In the end it is important how groups of required functionalities are implemented in a specific product, rather than the individual components. Indeed the less productized the CMS product is (high-end tool sets, or created using Zope) the more care needs to be taken in what the system has to enable and deliver.

The business plan contains the organization's vision of the benefits of implementing a CMS. Now the SoR must do the same for the CMS vendor. However, it must do so in a way that ensures that the evaluation process is fair (especially in a public sector environment), realistic and dependable, and so it has to be written in a way that facilitates the selection process from the outset.

This is where the personas and scenarios developed earlier in the project have a significant value, because they represent even more clearly than a list of functionalities what the organization believes the CMS will help it achieve.

The structure of the SoR

Some organizations have agreed a format for an SoR, and some thought will need to be given at the outset as to whether this format, either in part or in total, is appropriate to the purpose of selecting a CMS. The format that I have set out below is one that I have used on a number of occasions. In the end the exact structure does not matter so long as all the information that is required by a vendor (or a software house) is presented clearly and in appropriate depth.

Executive summary

An SoR document can be quite a substantial document, and preparing an executive summary can be valuable in ensuring that the key messages are contained in the body of the document, and link back to the original business case.

The organization

Organizations are complicated, and just sending a copy of the annual report as a means of providing background on the organization is a poor substitute for creating a section of the SoR that goes beyond the public view of the organization. There is obviously a need to maintain an appropriate level of confidentiality, but it can be very helpful to illustrate how the organization coped with any previous major IT application implementation. If a new library management application took much longer than anticipated to implement there may be a higher level of scrutiny of the CMS implementation to ensure that the situation does not arise a second time. An organization chart can be invaluable, especially if it is current!

The people

Over the period of the selection and implementation of the CMS there will be a small team of people from the organization working closely with the vendor. Providing some biographical information on the team can substantially enhance the level of communication between the vendor and the organization. Even if there are staff that are performing background roles (such as the procurement manager) a note of the name and role of these members of staff again can be of mutual benefit.

Business case

It can be useful to summarize the basis on which the business case was made, because this will provide the vendor with an understanding of the organizational dynamics, and more importantly the expectations that the organization has for the CMS. It may be that the vendor feels that these expectations are perhaps unrealistic, and that they need to be addressed in the response, or at least clarified at the outset of the process.

Content scenarios

This section should set out in some detail the core content-enabled business processes which have been set out in principle in the business case. The most important element is how, and by whom, content is added to the current website or intranet, and, ideally, how the organization wants this to change with a CMS. These processes might add information on new events to the website, adding project summaries to an intranet project database or publishing the annual report in HTML, pdf and RTF formats. It is useful to put some quantification into these descriptions, such as the number of documents, or the size of a typical project summary. Providing examples of the documents or content elements can be valuable, even if they are mocked-up for reasons of confidentiality.

A typical example is outlined in the following case study.

Case study: a Content Management scenario

We run around twenty conferences each year. Some are events that we run every year, and all that we need to do is to add in the changes of date, venue and speakers, but the basic programme structure remains unchanged. As well as publishing the brochure on the website we also publish and mail out a printed version of the brochure.

Each year we have a number of new events, and usually the programme brochure has to be developed from scratch. We include a number of graphics in each brochure, taken from our photographic library.

The process of developing the brochures for either the regular or new events involves a number of different departments. Each event has an Event Manager responsible for the programme, but the overall event has to be signed off by the Event Director. We tend to recruit new graduates as Event Managers, and they tend to move on quite quickly so we currently have a need to train people to use Dreamweaver on quite a regular basis.

Our Commercial Manager also has to review the brochure to make sure that the information on the registration form is clear and accurate. We also have a designer that works for us on a freelance basis. Some of our conferences are European in scope and this requires us to liaise with colleagues in a subsidiary company in France.

After the event we would like to make the presentations available to delegates. This is something that is difficult for use to do at present because the presentations are usually in PowerPoint and we do not want to mount large PowerPoint files on our server. We also have no means of ensuring that only bona fide delegates are able to register to download the documents.

This information would enable a prospective vendor to plan the proposal around:

- taking a sample of the conference brochure from the website and demonstrating the way in which the content could be edited, including managing the graphics
- a workflow branch to the designer, who may not be on the organization's e-mail directory
- the complex internal review process

- showing how different formats could be generated from the master version
- the substantial version control issue because the event programmes are probably built up paper by paper
- how support would be provided to the subsidiary in France, and what the licensing model might be, because the French operation might need only occasional access to the CMS
- current substantial training requirement and how the CMS would reduce this training load.

The aim should be to set out some of the main business processes where it is expected that implementing a CMS would have a significant business benefit. This section of the SoR should, of course, link back into the business case.

Implementation issues

Although it may be possible under some circumstances to roll out the CMS to all users over a short period of time, perhaps a few days, usually a CMS is implemented on a step-wise basis, as discussed in Chapter 11. At this stage of the project the factors that might influence the roll-out will have been well identified, and some project milestones agreed. This project plan should be set out in the SoR. It will enable the vendor to judge whether the company has the resources to meet these milestones. There may be another major implementation that has already been agreed, or key members of the vendor project team may be away on vacation.

There are also likely to be some important dates as far as the organization is concerned. A university academic year is a good example. Implementing a CMS during the September/October student registration period is likely to run into some resourcing problems. Upgrades of the IT and network platforms also need to be taken into consideration.

The most difficult aspect to forecast is the work involved in migrating content from the current systems to the CMS, and this is discussed in detail in Chapter 12.

ICT platform architecture

This section should set out in some detail the desktop environment, the network and server architecture, the preferred database environment and any issues about remote access.

Selection criteria

Any specific requirements (perhaps the ability to preview a page without checking the content back into the system) should be set clearly, giving reasons. This helps the vendor present solutions that play to their strengths, and also enables the vendor to see if the client really does understand the requirements of the organization and the way in which a CMS would be implemented. If a case cannot be made for the inclusion of a specific functionality then is it really that important to the selection process?

The selection criteria should be grouped under the topics set out in Chapter 2, and therefore would cover:

- content contribution
- workflow management
- content versioning
- content tagging
- content repurposing
- content publishing
- site management
- search
- administration.

A very effective way of developing the selection criteria is to use the *Content Management Requirements Toolkit* that has been developed by James Robertson of Step Two Designs, Sydney, Australia. The second edition of this *Toolkit* was released in August 2004; it sets out around 130 potential requirements for CMS products. For each requirement the *Toolkit* describes the key issues that need to be taken into consideration. The *Toolkit* is so comprehensive that there is little point in emulating it in this *Handbook*.

The *Toolkit* is published as a pdf file and an associated Word file so that relevant sections can be cut and pasted into a statement of requirements.

As an example of the approach, the section dealing with Workflow is set out in the shaded panel.

2.5 Workflow

There is a need to be able to manage content from initial drafts through to published pages, with reviews at set points in the process. These reviews may be done by a range of people throughout the organisation.

This editorial and content review will be critical to ensuring that the content of the site is both accurate and up-to-date.

2.5.1 Simple workflows

The content management system must provide simple and easy-to-use workflow which provides at least the following features:

- multiple status settings for content items, such as draft, in review, published, expired, etc.
- simple linear workflows with a limited number of steps
- capture of comments entered by reviewers

It should also be possible to either escalate workflow steps automatically, or notify the relevant author or administrator of a delay in the workflow process.

When reviewing or approving content, users should have the changes to the page highlighted visually, thereby making it much easier for the reviewer to assess the modifications.

2.5.2 Advanced workflows

Beyond basic workflow capabilities, the content management system will need to support a range of powerful features including:

- dynamic routing based on defined rules
- parallel workflows
- support for authorisation by staff groups, according to defined rules (majority, unanimous, etc)
- unlimited number of workflow steps
- automated initiation of activities at defined workflow steps (such as sending data to a third-party application)
- graphical views and editing of workflows

(*Continued on next page*)

(*Continued*)
The vendor should outline any other workflow capabilities, and indicate how these would assist in meeting the business goals of the project.

2.5.3 Workflow administration
The content management system must provide an interface that allows the local administrators to create and modify workflow rules, without requiring either technical knowledge or vendor assistance.
This includes:

- creating new workflows
- deleting of workflows
- updating roles or steps in existing workflows
- modifying conditional rules

2.5.4 Reports
The content management system should provide a range of reports to assist the administrators in managing the workflow processes. These should include summaries of the status of the workflows that have been initiated, as well as reports highlighting any overdue workflow steps.
The vendor must provide a detailed description of the workflow reports that are provided.

2.6 Integration with enterprise workflow engine
The organisation already has an enterprise-wide workflow engine that is used to manage business processes across a range of systems and platforms.
The vendor should outline how the content management system can be integrated with this workflow engine, to provide seamless interoperability with other business systems.

(Reprinted with permission from the *Content Management Requirements Toolkit*. See the Step Two Designs website (www.steptwo.com.au) for full details of this product.)

Just compiling an SoR by a global cut and paste of the *Content Management Requirements Toolkit* is not the only process for selecting a CMS. There are similar checklists in the *Content Management Bible* by Bob Boiko (2002) and in *Managing Enterprise*

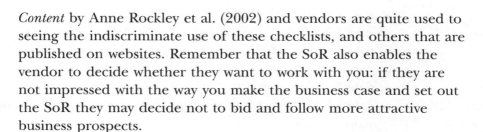
Content by Anne Rockley et al. (2002) and vendors are quite used to seeing the indiscriminate use of these checklists, and others that are published on websites. Remember that the SoR also enables the vendor to decide whether they want to work with you: if they are not impressed with the way you make the business case and set out the SoR they may decide not to bid and follow more attractive business prospects.

The most effective way to use one of these checklists is to go through each heading in detail and ask:

1 Do I understand the significance of the requirement? If not then further research is required. One way of deciding whether you do understand the significance is if you can convey the importance of the requirement to someone with no technical knowledge of a CMS.

2 Is the requirement
   — mandatory for the achievement of the objectives of the CMS?
   — very important?
   — useful, perhaps for a subsequent expansion or enhancement of the CMS?
   — of no relevance to the implementation?

The mandatory requirements should be clearly stated in the SoR so that companies that do not meet these requirements are excluded from consideration at the outset. For example:

> There should be a capability to use different style sheets for specific sections of the website and these style sheets can be edited using a user-friendly interface with no requirement to write new code for the sheets.

The selection process will then involve weighting and ranking the very important and useful criteria.

Selection process

The timetable for the selection process should be clearly set out, and cover:

- date for a meeting with prospective vendors
- date for receipt of proposals
- date when vendors are informed if they are shortlisted
- date(s) for the vendors to present their proposals
- date for a decision on a preferred vendor
- date when the organization could be in a position to support a scoping study
- date by when the organization intends to confirm the vendor.

This requires some careful forward planning, especially if the tender has to go through a public procurement route. The purpose of a tenderer meeting is to give the vendors the chance to clarify any specific issues in both an open meeting and in one-to-one meetings with the project staff. It also shows the vendors who else is being considered: sometimes vendors drop out when they see the nature of the competition.

This might not be to the advantage of the organization, as it may not lead to the best solution being found, and the reasons for the opt-out should always be explored. Any issues that come up in the one-to-one meetings that are of generic value to all the vendors should be circulated. The permission of the vendor who raised the issue should be sought, though in the end the decision of the project board should always be final.

Background information on the company

The questions raised need to be relevant to the organization and the vendor. I have seen an SoR that asked for the number of employees, and both BT and IBM gave the total number of UK employees, which had no impact on their ability to implement the system.

The key issues to explore are:

- the current trading position of the company
- the legal entity in the country of purchase
- number of staff with expertise of the product offered
- the current installed base
- the ratio between licence fees and consulting.

Another important issue is the extent to which the vendor uses third-party software. Some areas where this is common is in workflow software (Microsoft Visio is a favourite), text editors (Ektron for example) or search software (Verity or Convera). The vendor will not be in full control of these relationships, and a list of third-party software products that are embedded in the CMS product can be quite revealing.

Project management methodology

Effective project management is so important in the implementation phase that a check at this stage can give a very useful insight into just how the project will be managed, especially if a systems integrator is involved. One component of the methodology should be the skills and contribution that the vendor expects from the client.

Reference sites

Each vendor will have sites where everything seemed to go just fine. Sometimes this is because the customer is so important for reference purposes that the entire company was brought in to sort out the problems at no cost to the organization. The vendor should be asked to state the relevance of the reference site to the specific proposal, and not just present a cut-and-paste from another proposal. Make sure that the implementation is of the version of the software you will be buying unless you want to be at the leading edge, a.k.a. bleeding edge.

Managing the response

The organization needs to appoint a member of the team to deal with queries from vendors. It is useful (and in some public sector procurements mandatory) that a note is made of the query and how it is resolved. Many organizations circulate corrections and clarifications to an SoR based on the feedback. It important to be even-handed in the relationship with prospective vendors so that there are no suggestions of improper behaviour later.

Each vendor presents its response to the SoR in a different way, often putting in considerable amounts of background information on how wonderful the company is. You are only interested in transferable knowledge, i.e. knowledge gained that is relevant to you, and not just a list of every customer for the last three years. It may be quite a challenge to get the vendors to present their responses in a stipulated format, but it can be beneficial to ask them to send the responses as both electronic files and as hard copies.

It can be helpful to stipulate that there should be an executive summary of perhaps two pages that sets out a concise summary of the response, ideally keyed into the main document through paragraph numbers or page numbers. Not only does this enable the selection panel to gain an immediate view of the proposal without working through pages of fine print, but as the process of selection gets underway it also enables the team to recall the key features of a product that they might have worked through the day before, or even earlier.

If the document is in Microsoft Word it can be useful to turn on Track Changes and/or look at the Properties box to see if the tender is in fact just a modified version of one that was presented to another organization!

Summary

- Although it is important to understand the functionalities of CMS products just listing them and asking a vendor to tick the relevant boxes is a totally ineffectual way of selecting a vendor.
- More important than the individual components is how groups of required functionalities are implemented in a specific product.
- The aim should be to set out some of the main business processes where it is expected that implementing a CMS would have a significant business benefit.
- The SoR should ensure that the evaluation process is fair (especially in a public sector environment), realistic and dependable; it has to be written in a way that from the outset facilitates the selection process.

References

Boiko, B. (2002) *Content Management Bible*, New York, Hungry Minds.

Rockley, A., with Kostur, P. and Manning, S. (2002) *Managing Enterprise Content: a unified content strategy*, Indianapolis, New Riders, www.newriders.com.

The selection process

Introduction

A CMS has to be seen to be believed! An essential element of the selection process is to arrange for vendors on the short list to give a presentation of the way in which they plan to meet the objectives of the organization. This should not be the first time that the selection team has seen the product. The complexity of even entry-level products is such that even in a two-hour presentation only a relatively few features of the CMS will be covered. To be useful the vendor presentations have to be managed with military precision, and require as much commitment from the project team as any other element of the procurement process. The words 'demonstration' and 'presentation' are used with specific meaning. Vendors are good at demonstrating how good their product is at doing the things that it is good at. The challenge of a presentation is to make sure that the product does all the things that the organization requires within specific business, technology and organizational constraints.

At the heart of the evaluation process should be the personas and scenarios set out in the statement of requirements. At the present time vendors are not yet as comfortable with this approach to meeting requirements as they will need to become.

How many vendors?

In deciding how many vendors to place on a short list, and then invite to give a demonstration, the time required to watch the presentation and to discuss the findings has to be taken into account. At this stage of the process there should perhaps be no more than four, or five at the outside. If the short list is still a long list, with more than five vendors, then there should be a re-evaluation of the written proposals.

One practical reason for setting the number at four is that ideally each vendor should be allocated one day for the presentation. The presentation itself should take only a couple of hours (see below) but there will no doubt be questions raised that take more time. The review by the project team should take place immediately after the presentation. If a series of presentations is held on the same day then there is the real danger that there will be confusion about which product presentation covers which features. Such is the impact of the CMS on the business effectiveness of the organization that allocating anything less than a day devalues the entire process.

Assessing the written proposals

The tender documents themselves can provide important information that will assist with the vendor selection, and it is well worth reading them carefully to see what has been omitted or glossed over:

- The sales team may have cut and pasted text from an earlier proposal and not fully checked to make sure that the details are consistent and accurate.
- Particular care needs to be taken with information about reference clients. It is worth checking that the vendor has actually carried out the work. Some CMS vendors have reference sites that their software integration partners can use in their proposals with the intention of demonstrating the capabilities of the software. It may not be either clear whether the partner themselves has actually carried out the work.

The tender document should also be taken as an illustration of the way in which the project documentation will be presented:

- If the tender is a mix of different styles, with an inadequate index and a variable approach to paragraph formatting perhaps the project documentation will look the same, and be equally as difficult to assimilate.
- Tenders are often padded out with irrelevant information, such as the unedited C.V.s of members of the project team or the history of the company.

- There is little point in padding out the tender document with copies of the annual filings of the company when only one member of the selection panel will be able to interpret them.

This is why it is essential to set out in the statement of requirements just how the tender should be prepared and submitted.

Developing the short list

The selection criteria should be set out in a way that enables the selection panel to quite quickly reduce the number of vendors down to a manageable total. Certainly there ought to be four or five on the short list, but probably no more than that. The process of the detailed evaluation, vendor presentations and subsequent meetings to clarify details is quite time consuming enough without extending the process to ten or more vendors.

If the short list is indeed as long as ten then the initial selection criteria, and arguably the original statement of requirements, were probably not rigorous enough. That, however, is water under the bridge, and an effort should be made to reduce the 'long' short list of ten to a 'short' short list of four or five. If the selection process has involved the use of a Government-approved list of vendors, or an advertisement in the Official Journal of the European Commission, then there might be fifty or more tenders to work through. The only way to manage this is to have a very clear idea of just a few top-level selection criteria.

Weighting and ranking selection criteria

At the heart of the formal evaluation process is the initial development of a weighted list of functionalities and other criteria. There is no point at all in just listing functionalities and then seeing how many each vendor can comply with.

How many criteria are used in the evaluation depends on the risk that could be associated with the vendor in fact failing to meet the one of the criteria. If for each of the criteria there is a short statement about the impact of the lack or achievement of the criterion on the success of the implementation then this process will substantially reduce the overall risk of the project.

The process involves getting the selection panel to agree on the selection criteria. These could be the use of XML, the approach to migration of legacy content, and the ease with which templates can be modified. Mandatory criteria will probably be budget, and the confidence the vendor has in meeting the implementation dates. However, neither can be evaluated on the basis of the initial proposals.

The relative importance of these criteria is then weighted on a scale of 1 to 4 (4 being mandatory). As each vendor comes in to make their pitch the panel gives them a ranking of 1 (no idea) to 5 (meets the requirement completely). Multiplying and summing the ranking and weighting scores produces an overall score for the vendor.

An example for the purposes of illustration only is given below in Table 10.1.

Table 10.1 Illustration of a weighted and ranked evaluation of vendors

Requirement	Weight	Vendor A score	Vendor A Rank	Vendor B score	Vendor B Rank	Vendor C score	Vendor C Rank
Dual Novell Groupwise and Microsoft Active Directory support	4	5	20	5	20	5	20
Support for e-Government Metadata Standard	4	5	20	5	20	4	16
Apply metadata based on content type	3	5	15	4	12	1	3
Complete site roll back	3	2	6	3	9	2	6
Existing clients in local government on same version	3	2	6	2	6	5	15
Creation of documents in pdf format	3	3	9	2	6	5	15
Server-based licensing	2	4	8	2	4	2	4
Templates easily developed by the client	2	4	8	3	6	4	8
Total			92		83		87

Note: The requirements are purely illustrative

It is important not to place too much reliance in the final score. The benefits of this approach are in the discussions around the initial selection criteria, and the allocation or the weighting and ranking scores. The process should ensure that all (or at least most) hidden agendas are revealed, and that perhaps one of the criteria needs to be split into two.

It may well be the case that there is some ambiguity in the statement of requirements, so that some of the vendors may have interpreted the requirement in one way, and some in another. If this is the case then the ambiguity needs to be resolved and the outcome communicated to all the vendors.

At the end of the process the outcome should be four or at most five vendors. A decision needs to be made as to whether the unsuccessful vendors are told why they have not made the short list. There may be a rule in the procurement process that requires this to be done.

Open-source CMS

With the growing interest in, and availability of, open-source software this might be one of the options to be considered in the evaluation process. If the open-source software has been productized then the product can be assessed against commercial products, but if there is only a proposal from the IT department to build a CMS using open-source software the selection process will be like comparing apples and oranges.

This is where a focus on what the software can deliver in terms of a finished CMS rather than on the functionality of the software is absolutely essential. By using the support networks for the software, organizations that have similar requirements to those set out in the SoR can be identified and visits made to these organizations at the outset of the process to understand how the software has been developed, and the problems during the development process and implementation.

The selection panel

Much of the work to this point has been carried out by the CMS project team. Now is the time to broaden the team to include other stakeholders. The selection panel should comprise:

1 the CMS project manager, for obvious reasons
2 an experienced content author who can ask questions about the authoring interface, metadata management, etc.
3 a representative from IT with both server and network knowledge. The network knowledge is essential where the CMS is to be integrated into a corporate network through the network directory, with appropriate permissions based on the network security model
4 the senior manager who is sponsoring the project, to show the vendor that a key decision maker has taken the time to be present
5 if appropriate, a representaive from the procurement department to ensure that organization rules about the procurement process are complied with.

A panel of five is quite large enough. The panel has to be consistent throughout the presentations. There has to be comparability, and if three different IT staff turn up to the presentations that will be lost. Getting all these people in the same room at the same time, and at a time when the vendors can also be present with the appropriate personnel is the main reason why the vendor presentation stage can extend the overall schedule at a critical point of the procurement process.

Roles of the selection panel

Each member of the panel should be briefed on the points they need to watch out for, based on prior demonstrations. A set of agreed questions should also be developed, so that every member of the panel is involved in the process. It is quite easy to fall asleep in a CMS presentation! As well as what panel members say it is also important to manage what they don't say, especially in a public-sector procurement situation. The best way to do this is agree that only the CMS project manager will speak about any issues other than the agreed questions.

The selection criteria used for the development of the short list will almost certainly need to be modified for use in arriving at the choice of vendor. This is because the emphasis needs to shift from what the product does to how well it does it. Even in a pre-planned presentation it should be quite easy to see how quickly (for example) metadata can be added to a piece of content.

Another factor that needs to be considered in the evaluation process is how well the organization feels it can work with the vendor. It is unlikely that the vendor can confirm and have in attendance the project manager for the CMS implementation but it is important to take account of how well the team members work with each other, how well the questions are dealt with, and the overall level of personal commitment that is in evidence to working effectively with the organization.

Preparing for the presentation

Room – The choice of rooms is critical. The main room should have good ventilation, and the screen should be in a position where everyone in the room can see it, without image resolution being impacted by sunshine. There should also be an adjacent room where the selection panel can wait for the vendor to prepare the presentation, and where the panel can retire to, either at the end of the presentation or if there is a need to take 'time out' during the presentation because of an issue or problem that has arisen.

Equipment – The vendor's requirements for power sockets and internet connections should be established in good time. The weak link in a presentation is often the data projector, which is either noisy or has insufficient power for a large room. A back-up projector has to be available, even if it means hiring one. The project schedule will be quite tight enough without having to rerun a presentation because the data projector failed. Having a flip chart available can also be helpful to capture specific pieces of information.

Recording the presentation – It may also be work considering videoing the presentations, so that at the end of the week memories can be refreshed about just what was said in response to a specific question. The agreement of the vendor should be sought in advance, and a commitment made to send the tape back to the vendor at the conclusion of the review. In that way the vendor is able to use the tape for training purposes and also knows that it will not be used at the staff party for amusement.

It is essential that the presentation is not just a generic sales pitch, and this can be avoided by providing each vendor with some sample documents and style sheets. In the case of a website the vendor will be quite capable of grabbing style sheet information from the public website, but will not have this opportunity in the case of an intranet.

On the day

The timing of the presentation should be clearly set out in writing to the vendors. The shaded panel opposite gives an example.

The review process

Taking into account all that has been learned over a period of perhaps several days requires time and good leadership. The irony is that the work that has been carried out in defining the requirements and in selecting the short list means that the differences between the vendors are quite small and not directly comparable. One vendor may have a very good text editor and another a very user-friendly metadata tagger.

Visits to reference sites

At this stage visiting some reference sites can help in deciding between closely matched vendors. However, there is sometimes a reluctance on the part of vendors to be too accommodating with regard to visits to reference sites. Obviously the sites themselves do not want to have their work disrupted on a regular basis so the vendor will look for a strong commitment to purchase before setting up one meeting, let alone two.

They will almost certainly want to be closely involved in the site visits because their client could be facing difficulties which are in fact due to a lack of understanding of the CMS software rather than any fundamental flaw in the CMS.

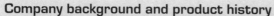

Company background and product history 10 minutes

You should watch for the extent to which this initial section of the presentation is tuned to the needs of the organization.

Meeting the scenario requirements 50 minutes

The statement of requirements (Chapter 9) sets out some scenarios for content authoring and publishing, and it is these scenarios that form the basis for the evaluation of the CMS product. This section must not be rushed, because meeting the scenario requirements lies at the heart of the selection process.

Initial questions 10 minutes

It is tempting to ask questions during the presentation, but this should be avoided because it is easy to then skip over a process in the desire to stay on track. This is where a video record can be very useful, because a particular process can be reviewed in the break-out session and specific questions asked within the overall context of the presentation.

Other product features 30 minutes

The scenario presentations will give the vendor a chance to show only a comparatively small but important number of features. This next period of time can be used by the vendor to show other features that, based on their response to the statement of requirements, gives them a competitive advantage. This section of the presentation should also cover the vendor's approach to project management.

Break out 30 minutes

After 90 minutes everyone will need a break. The selection panel should use this time to discuss the outcomes of the presentation, agree the list of questions that need to be raised, and also agree who will ask each question.

Questions 30 minutes

Vendor recapitulation 20 minutes

The presentation has taken over two hours, assuming that everything has run to plan. It can be valuable to give the vendor a chance to summarize why they offer the best solution to the needs of the organization.

How much?

Even at this stage it is unlikely that there will be a commitment to a price from the vendor. The lower the level of customization involved the easier it is for the vendor to be forthcoming about the licence cost and any associated professional services for template design, technical implementation and training. As the functionality of the product increases so does the difficulty for the vendor in providing a firm quotation. The problem is more acute with open-source software, where the licence fee may be zero or minimal, and all the costs are in the development work involved.

Scoping study

The next step with most vendors is to undertake what is often referred to as a 'scoping study'. This is a short project, typically a week in duration, during which time consultants from the vendor look in considerable detail at the IT platforms, network architecture and server architecture, and also at the current website or intranet. The objective is to quantify the licence fee and the professional services work that will be involved in the implementation.

The cost of the scoping study usually has to be borne by the organization, because at this stage there is no commitment to proceed with the vendor concerned. Some vendors undertake the work at no cost if the contract is then placed with them, but reserve the right to charge if this is not the case. The vendor will also stipulate that the report of the scoping study cannot be passed on to a third party, such as another prospective vendor.

Once this work has been completed the vendor is in a position to confirm the price of the software and implementation, but rarely will this be a fixed-price quotation. Certainly the software licence element will be but any professional services work will be priced on a day-rate basis so that unforeseen problems (especially content migration) can be charged for at cost.

Organizations like to have fixed-price quotations, and indeed may not be able to enter into what is often referred to as a time and materials contract under their internal procurement rules.

One of the outcomes of the scoping study is that the organization feels that the vendor will not be able to meet their requirements, and that is why it is important to have a vendor in reserve. However, it may well be that the second-place vendor is there because they are the best of the rest, rather than being a close call with the vendor of preference. At this point a substantial amount of courage is needed within the organization to decide that the gap between the statement of requirements is so wide in critical areas that the process should not proceed to selection, but rather that the project team should go back to the statement of requirements and look again at the requirements and the criteria for selection.

Contract negotiation

The conflict between the ambition on the part of the organization to agree a fixed-price contract and the reluctance of the vendor to do so makes the negotiation of the contract a potentially difficult and time-consuming business. The vendor wishes to minimize their risk and maximize their profit, and finding a compromise can be quite a challenge.

Feedback

A decision must be made as to the extent of any feedback that is provided to the unsuccessful vendors. Depending on the procurement rules of the organization, written feedback may be either mandatory or forbidden. If there is to be feedback it is important to state the nature of the feedback in the statement of requirements. This could range from a letter indicating the main reasons for not selecting the CMS to a copy of the formal evaluation of the CMS. The requirements of any Freedom of Information legislation, especially in the UK and the USA, need to be taken into consideration. There may be grounds for vendors applying under this legislation to have a copy of the evaluation report so that they can be satisfied that the procedure does conform to the procurement policies of the organization.

Summary

- Vendors are good at demonstrating how good their product is at doing the things that it is good at. The challenge of a presentation is to make sure that the product does all the things that the organization requires within specific business, technology and organizational constraints.

- At the heart of the evaluation process should be the personas and scenarios that are set out in the statement of requirements.

- The short list is made after the initial development of a weighted list of functionalities and other criteria. There is no point at all in just listing functionalities and then seeing how many each vendor can comply with.

- Even at this stage it is unlikely that there will be a commitment to a price from the vendor.

Implementation

Introduction

The implementation of a CMS starts at the time the statement of requirements is being written and not when the date for the installation of the software is agreed. The main reason for this is that the implementation of a CMS is about people and processes, and not about technology. Even a small change in a process can have a significant impact on an individual or a team, and these changes need to be considered at the outset of the project, because they cannot be rushed.

Each implementation is unique

It is difficult to generalize about the complexity and duration of an implementation. If the website is well structured and the information architecture and metadata are to remain the same, then the implementation may take only a few weeks at the outside. The problems tend to emerge when an intranet is involved, because in general the number of authors will be greater and the processes will be embedded into ongoing business activities which, being part of a chain of such processes, may not be easy to change on an ad hoc basis.

Because the implementation is specific to the organization concerned it is dangerous to place too much reliance on the claims of the vendor about how long it took in 'an organization just like yours'. There are no other organizations just like yours, because of the people factor. Like all software, CMS applications are really quite stupid. They run on a set of rules and assume that people using the software also run on a set of rules. Most of the time that might be the case, but it is when the rules need to be changed that the ability of the software to accommodate these changes starts to be challenged. It is difficult to test these out prior to implementation. Even if it is possible to use a test suite or pilot implementation to see how best to add course information to the website ensuring that it is scalable for all departments, courses and the skills of individual authors will only emerge in due course.

Managing stakeholder interests

The implementation of a CMS touches a lot of people in the organization, and outside, and managing these requires skilful project management and people management.

Typical stakeholders are listed in Table 11.1.

Table 11.1 Stakeholders in CMS implementation

Stakeholder	Concerns
Project sponsor	Will the CMS deliver the expected benefits to the organization?
	Will the project stay inside budget?
	Has the project manager thought of all the things that could go wrong?
	What happens if we fail to meet the schedule?
Project manager	Is the project plan sound?
	If we need more resources or change the schedule will I get support from the organization?
	Will I know when the vendor is being 'economical with the truth'?
	Will the migration of the legacy content go to plan?
CMS vendor	Will we be able to use this implementation as a reference site?
	Does the project manager really know what they are doing?
	Have we bid the project at a level that will achieve our profit margins?
IT department	How much support must we allocate to this project?
	Will our servers and networks be adequate to support the level of use?
	What impact will the CMS have on the integrity of our IT platforms?
Department manager	What will be the impact on staff training?
	If I have to defer the implementation for the department when will I be able to get back onto the implementation plan?
Web author	How long will it take me to become familiar with the software?
	What changes will take place to the way in which content is authored and published?
Prospective web author	How much training will I need?
	Will I get support from my manager?

Table 11.1 is only a summary of the concerns, and it is important for the organization, and in particular the project manager and the sponsor, to have a clear view of what these concerns are both at the outset of the project and as it proceeds. There may be a problem with the implementation in one department so that the word gets round that things are much more difficult than everyone has been led to believe and resistance starts to build up in other departments. Bad news always travels faster than good news in an organization.

Project communication

Communications within the implementation process should be the subject of a well considered plan. If there is an internal communications department then the expertise is already available, but if not then a member of the project team must take responsibility for devising and implementing a communications strategy. The elements of this strategy will be rather different for a website than an intranet, with the latter presenting the greater challenge.

Communication channels

As with the project itself the communications strategy needs to start as soon as a firm decision is taken to proceed with a CMS. It is all about managing expectations: there must be a balance between the vision of what the CMS means to the organization and the detail of what is about to happen next. The communications channels should be as diverse and appropriate as possible, and might include:

- individual and group meetings with senior managers to brief them on progress and act as a forum for feedback
- a section of the current intranet, used as a project site. (This could use inexpensive blog software to provide a diary of the progress of the project. Some blog software products include a Comments channel which might facilitate 'two-way' communication with staff.)
- a wiki site so that a set of FAQs about the project can be published and revised with the minimum of effort and delay

- staff newsletters and meetings for more general presentations on the progress of the project
- a specific name for the implementation project so that it is easy to refer to it in conversations and meetings.

Feedback

Whatever the approaches used there should be good feedback channels. A CMS implementation is a novel experience and the better the quality and timeliness of the feedback from all the stakeholders the more likely the overall success of the project. It is important to include the vendors and other implementation staff in the communications strategy because they are in the front line of dealing with staff. Make sure that there are brief biographies of the vendor staff available: this will help the process of implementation quite significantly.

Working with the vendor

The vendor's implementation team should not only be aware of the way in which the progress of the project is being communicated but should also be involved in the process of deciding what messages need to be communicated. Nothing is more likely to cause internal problems than the organization saying that the new site will go live on 14 September and the vendor implementation team indicating that they will be on site until 30 September. There may be a simple answer to the apparent difference in dates, but this needs to be communicated clearly to all involved in the implementation process.

Changing job descriptions

It happens less with websites, but certainly with intranets the authorship of pages is all too often seen as a hobby, or something that does not take long at all and can be fitted around ongoing work. The result is that when faced with two tasks – one in their job description and web work that is not – a member of staff will defer the web work. Content is then not added in a timely fashion and there is a real danger that the investment in the CMS will not have the impact expected.

It is difficult to change job descriptions at a stroke, because it is not immediately clear what the job involves in terms of skills and experience. Furthermore, if web authoring is added to the job description what is left off? The involvement of the HR department from the outset of the project is essential. It may well take the time from the writing of the SoR to the conclusion of the implementation for issues around job descriptions and grading to be resolved. Linked with any changes to job descriptions are training requirements. At the outset of the implementation, training is rightly given a high priority, but then tends to fall off the training agenda. However, staff will join the company or move to new jobs within the company, so the training requirements have to be upgraded on a permanent basis.

Training requirements

The training requirements are not limited to the use of the CMS. Just as important is teaching staff how to write for web applications; this includes staff who think they know all about it. Even if the training on the CMS application cannot start until the software has been installed training on effective writing for the web can start at the very outset of the project.

If web content has been the responsibility of a small core team then considerable attention needs to be paid to the training of new authors who will contribute content for the first time. Even where there is already a degree of decentralized content contribution it is unwise to assume that these authors have a consistent level of awareness and expertise in web authoring,

In decentralized situations authors tend to fall between two ends of a spectrum:

- technically qualified in using, for example, FrontPage or Dreamweaver but with little knowledge of the work of the department; they take content that has been written within the department and create new or revised web pages
- very familiar with the work of the department and able to write excellent content but have only a very limited expertise in web design and are using only the basic facilities of FrontPage, or just one or two templates

The training requirements of these two cadres are quite different, and the type of training, the cost and the time when the training should be undertaken, all have to be taken into consideration. Should the training be through attendance at commercial courses or developed especially for the organization?

The training programme does not stop on the day that the CMS is implemented. Content authors will leave or take on different responsibilities; there will be a continuing requirement for training in both web skills and in the CMS itself. Although the CMS will take away the need for technical skills (at least to a substantial extent) using CMS templates does not mean that the content is well written or reliable. That has to come through training and ongoing review of the content being added to the system.

Site design

The design of the site should be agreed in outline during the development of the business case, and in more detail as the statement of requirements is written. The idea that this work can wait until the CMS software actually arrives is not a sensible one. The process of website design is an iterative one that calls for consultation and testing. The design has an impact on the way that metadata are developed and on the content that needs to be migrated or written before the site goes live.

It is often believed that once the CMS is installed it is much easier to change the design if it is found not to be optimum on launch. This is true to only a very limited extent:

- The work involved in implementing templates and style sheets in a CMS can be quite resource-intensive.
- Users will expect a substantial improvement in the usability and findability of the site. If these expectations are not met then constant modifications to the site annoy rather than impress.
- A small change on one page may have quite an unforeseen implication elsewhere on the site.

Usability testing

A continuous element of the implementation should be usability testing. This has already been covered as far as the design stage has been concerned in Chapter 11. Usability testing is essential and not an option. One of the benefits of devising the SoR in terms of scenarios is that these can be converted into user tests that relate directly to the core processes of the organization. There are many excellent books and workshops on usability testing so setting out how to carry out the tests is not appropriate here. What does need to be taken into account is how the usability tests are going to fit into the overall implementation. Good usability tests take time to carry out, and then time needs to be allowed in the project plan for remedial action to be carried out before the project proceeds.

Accessibility

This term is usually applied to the design of websites to ensure that as far as possible they are usable by visitors and staff who have either visual or physical disabilities. The level of compliance is still low, according to a number of surveys, and the redesign of a site as part of the CMS implementation process gives an excellent opportunity to make a website or an intranet compliant.

In a CMS implementation there is a another aspect of accessibility to consider, and that is the extent to which the CMS authoring interface can be used by authors who may have visual or physical disabilities. There could well be a situation where a member of staff with such a disability is contributing content as a Word file that they are forwarding to the web team for inclusion on the site, especially for an intranet. Providing them with access to the CMS may result in some issues about accessibility. Vendors are paying attention to these issues now, but no surveys have been carried out to discover the extent to which the software meets Web Accessibility Initiative (WAI) and other accessibility standards. It should be called for in the SoR and verified as the implementation progresses.

Content migration

Content migration is such an important subject that it is covered in depth in Chapter 12. It is included here to ensure that the issues about the uncertainties of legacy migration are included in the project plan.

Roll-out strategies

Rolling out a CMS solution to the entire organization in one step is a very risky exercise unless the organization is quite small and the number of authors is small. There is no one ideal roll-out strategy, and each has its advantages and challenges. Some of the issues to consider are the following:

Importance of the business process

If the objective of the implementation is to be able to update a list of public training courses and conferences on the website then that would seem to be the obvious place to focus the effort. The impact on the business will be immediate and significant, which will not only encourage all involved with the project but also result in some positive reactions from visitors to the site. In an intranet situation the core process may be less easy to determine because of the richness of the content on the site.

The major problem with this approach is that if there are any delays in the release of this element of the site then the entire project might be seriously derailed. One of the applications that is often a justification for a CMS is to enable visitors to register and gain access to content that meets their specific interests. This type of application also involves synchronizing the development of a customer database and some online form management. In general any deployment that involves two applications (i.e. CMS and customer registration database) being ready at the same time is a high risk and the downsides need to be realistically acknowledged.

Enthusiastic early adopter

In every organization there is usually one department or even one person who wants to be the early adopter, either because of their personal interest and commitment to the project, or because of support from the department manager. Having enthusiastic people working on a pilot project creates enthusiasm in the team working on it. On the other hand, an assessment must be made about the extent to which the lessons learned in this department are scalable to the rest of the organization. It could be that the public relations department, already skilled in the use of the web, wants to launch

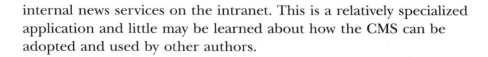

internal news services on the intranet. This is a relatively specialized application and little may be learned about how the CMS can be adopted and used by other authors.

Content similarity

In a distributed organization there might be IT support teams or HR departments in every subsidiary or location. They will have common content and, as support departments, will have information that is of interest to most users of an intranet. Once more detailed research is carried out it may well be found that not all such departments are the same, and that from a resourcing viewpoint one or more of the departments will have significant problems in either migrating legacy content or developing new content. The situation then becomes a 'weakest link in the chain' problem. Is the launch of the other departments delayed until all have reached a common level of content commitment, or do the departments launch as they are ready, putting a lot of pressure on departments which for good reasons are not able to be part of the initial round of site releases?

Search development

In the focus on implementing the CMS itself there is a danger that less attention is paid to the implementation of the search software, especially if it is a third-party product and perhaps one that the CMS vendor does not fully support. Apart from the integration of the search screens into the site design attention needs to be paid to making sure that the relevance rankings are appropriate for the content to be searched. To do this requires a representative sample of data to be available, which comes back to the problem of migrating legacy content and applying new metadata to the pages. Since it is rare for either a website or an intranet to have a full-featured search engine ahead of implementing a CMS there will be little experience to build on in developing weightings and relevance rankings.

The opportunity may be taken to adopt a 'best bets' approach to findability, where the library and/or intranet teams identify core content that is positioned at the top of the search results, an approach that Microsoft has adopted with success. Again the team needs access to the appropriate content to develop the best bets, and this work needs to be carefully scheduled around the ongoing CMS implementation.

Managing risks and problems

The importance of developing a risk analysis was emphasized in Chapter 8. This risk analysis needs to be updated on a regular basis, and not just written and filed away. Even in quite straightforward implementations unforeseen problems arise. In many cases these tend to be the result of communications problems between the various contractors involved, especially if a systems integrator is managing the dual implementation of a CMS and search software.

The progress of the project needs to be tracked on virtually a daily basis, and this is why it is difficult for the web manager to undertake the project management role as well as maintain the website. There should be documented procedures for:

- identifying the real nature of the problem
- agreeing who is responsible for resolving the problem
- resolving the problem itself
- understanding if the problem is a one-off or whether a similar situation will arise later in the project
- learning from the solution and so reducing the risk.

Summary

- The implementation of a CMS starts at the time the statement of requirements is written and not when the date for the installation of the software is agreed.
- Rolling out a CMS solution to the entire organization in one go is a very risky exercise unless the organization is quite small and the number of authors is small.
- There is no one ideal roll-out strategy, and each has its advantages and challenges.
- The implementation of a CMS touches a lot of people in the organization, and outside, and managing these requires skilful project management and people management.
- Communications within the implementation process should be the subject of a well considered plan.

12 Content migration

Introduction

One of the most difficult challenges in implementing a CMS is the migration of content from the existing site to the CMS. The reason is that at the outset of the project there may be little knowledge about even the number of pages that may be involved without beginning to take into consideration the variations in page design. One of the rationales behind the CMS implementation is to provide a more consistent look and feel to the site even when multiple authors are involved in site creation. The templates within a CMS will certainly be able to accomplish this going forward, but without a substantial transfer of legacy content the site will be worthless as an information resource.

In this *Handbook* content migration comes as almost the final chapter, because it is a process that is associated with the implementation of a CMS, but the reality is that the issues of content migration need to be considered at the outset, which is why undertaking a content audit is covered in Chapter 4. The migration process can have a significant impact on implementation costs, resources and project milestones but cannot be undertaken in practice until the CMS implementation is stable enough to either begin manual migration or to implement content migration software.

Content migration software

Issues concerning content migration systems stem from the fact that very rarely is the process just the transfer of content from the existing system to the CMS-based system. Associated with the migration process are:

- changes in the links to content because it is now in new locations
- addition of metadata, usually almost entirely absent in flat-file websites
- changes in the text of the content to reflect new standards on, for example, acronyms and departmental names
- changing directory-type pages from flat-file to database, requiring the development of databases and the conversion of the information on the pages to a database format.

A number of companies offer software products that support content migration, among them Vamosa (www.vamosa.com) and Nahava (www.nahava.com).

As is the case with classification software these products are not a complete solution, and there is as much variation between them as there is with CMS products. The selection of one of these products also depends on the CMS selected because it has to deal with the tagging that has been applied to the pages. During the next few years the migration solutions will become more powerful and CMS vendors will gain more experience in working with the migration software companies; the problems will decrease, but a totally automated solution is unlikely to appear for some years.

Metadata management

The focus of the current migration software solutions is the transfer of content from the legacy site to the CMS through a form of automated cut-and-paste. The ability to apply metadata tags and to insert new links is often severely limited. A factor that needs to be taken into account is the management of the process as far as the migration software and CMS software vendors are concerned. If the automated element of the process fails to achieve the results anticipated then there may be quite a problem in working out whether the problem lies with the migration software or the connectivity with the CMS software. Unravelling that could take a lot of patient detective work and could have an impact on the implementation schedule.

There are three issues to consider when evaluating these products:

- Will the product work with the particular range of content on the existing site?
- To what extent can it be used with specific CMS products? At the time of writing the Metalogix product (www.metalogix.net) is only suitable for Microsoft Content Server.
- How can the product be checked on an incremental basis, rather than trusting to luck and software? There must be a set of test data that can be migrated across into the new CMS where the degree of successful migration can be assessed.

There is one problem that currently is very difficult to address. All these CM migration products depend on there being a stable CMS environment, so the process of migrating the test file cannot begin until the CMS has been loaded and developed. This is not the time to discover that the performance of the migration software is not as high as was anticipated, in good faith, by the vendor, and that there is still a significant amount of manual migration and checking to undertake.

Test procedures

Developing the specification for the test file needs to be undertaken with some care, as it should be representative of the range of content problems that are likely to be encountered on the site. However this approach on its own will not give a sense of the accuracy of the software on the predominant content types on the site. Creating two test files is advisable. One will check on the range of content types and authoring software, and the second should contain perhaps 1000 pages of fairly standard content. This latter file will then give a sense of the speed of conversion and the types of pages that thrown up an exception report from the software.

The pricing basis for the software also needs to be taken into consideration. Some products offer a server-based license, and others use a page-migrated pricing structure. A comparison of the available products can not be made until there is a very dependable audit of the content that enables the likely costs of any page-based solution to be quantified.

Legacy content analysis

The process of managing the migration starts with the establishment of some ground rules on what will be migrated to the CMS. A substantial amount of legacy content may be pdfs of handbooks, policies and other content that need to be available, but do not need to be reformatted or rewritten for the CMS. The extent to which metadata need to be added to these files needs to be considered in the light of the search engine involved, and the likely demand for this information on a regular basis. It might be possible to dump many of these files in a folder called 'HR Policies 1997–2001' and accept that anyone needing one of these policies must take time and effort to look through the folder.

Content review

The process of content migration should be seen as an opportunity to reduce the amount of irrelevant information on the site, including inadvertent duplication. Typically in a university every department feels it needs a map of the campus showing the location of the building; without some control from the web team there can be a number of different maps, few of which are kept up to date to show new buildings or access routes. An essential element of the migration strategy should be to agree a set of common documents that each author can then use as required. This seems quite a simple task in principle but in reality (and to use the example of the maps) every department will feel that its map is the ideal one to be selected as the common document.

An important factor to consider is the extent to which the web team has been able to control the way in which pages have been authored. In the case of a website, and often in intranets, the web team has been responsible for adding the content to the site. This should mean that there is considerable consistency in the way that the content has been coded, and usually a single page-authoring software package has been in use for some time. The problem is far more difficult to address when there are multiple intranets, each developed using a range of different software tools, and with little or no consistency in the way these tools have been used.

Migration strategy

The development of a migration strategy needs to be accomplished in both a top-down and bottom-up way. The bottom-up approach involves working with content owners (who may of course not be content authors) about the content they are responsible for. In an intranet environment, where content ownership and authorship can shift between staff on a frequent basis, it may be quite difficult to track down staff who actually know what the department has produced, how current it is, and how much work might be needed to repurpose the content for the CMS.

There should also be a top-down approach. In Chapter 3 the concept of personas was presented as a way of developing an information architecture and a set of objectives for the website or intranet. The personas can also be used to define whether content should be migrated at the launch of the CMS or over a defined period of time to ensure that the information requirements set out in the personas can be met.

There will almost certainly be a gap in the middle where there is no consensus on the value of content, but at least some guidelines can be established through this process about the extent of the initial migration and what then needs to be achieved by specified dates in the future.

The migration strategy needs to be agreed as early in the overall schedule as the business plan, because the scale of the process has a substantial impact on:

- direct costs of acquiring content migration software
- the selection of the CMS vendor, because certain migration products only work with a Microsoft platform
- the development of metadata schemas
- the staff resources available to undertake the migration
- the risk management of the project, because the full extent of migration issues may not be apparent until quite late in the project schedule.

Quantifying resources

The processes of reviewing the content to assess whether it should be transferred to the CMS can start as soon as the migration strategy is agreed; given the pressure on the project once the CMS is actually installed the more work that can be accomplished in the early stages of the project the better. This work should also start to generate some metrics for the process, with some indicative process times for cutting and pasting text being developed. It takes time to open up a page, review it, and then cut and paste the content into another file format, even if this is only done on a test basis with the pasting of the copy into a Word template.

The basic formula is quite straightforward:

$$\frac{\text{Number of pages} \times \text{migration time in minutes}}{360}$$

The migration time has to include finding the page, reading and assessing it, pasting it into a new file, saving the file, closing down the web page and noting that the page has been processed. The factor of 360 is based on a six-hour day, because doing this work without some reasonable breaks and allowing time to deal with queries means that non-stop migration over an eight-hour day is not realistic. That formula seems innocuous until you use it to calculate the time for a 200,000 page site, and make the assumption that each page takes two minutes to process, without any new metadata being added. The result is around three person years of work. To look at it another way, if this work has to be accomplished in a two-month period then some 20 staff are needed on a continuous basis.

In addition, the migration work must be checked, and this needs to be carried out with a high degree of diligence throughout the process. It could well be the case that some initial migration work goes well and needs little remedial work, so the level of checking is reduced as the senior project staff continue working on other aspects of the CMS implementation. The danger then is that the migration team moves on to a different section of the site where there are some unforeseen migration issues and the checking process does not pick up these issues until so late in the process that the work may have to be redone.

The process of checking and then undertaking remedial work has to be factored into the time that needs to be allowed for content migration.

Summary

- Do not leave consideration of content migration until the CMS implementation stage. The scale of the migration process should be established at the outset of the project through the content audit of the current site.
- If the new site requires a substantial amount of content migration from the current site then no matter how good the CMS software is at managing the creation of new content the site will not be operational and useful until the migration has been undertaken.
- Although there is an increasing number of software solutions coming onto the market they are not a total solution, and there will still be a need for human intervention and checking.

13 Resources

Introduction

In this chapter a range of books, reports and websites on all aspects of content management are listed and reviewed. The links were checked in late 2004.

Books

Addey, D., Ellis, J., Suh, P. and Thiemecke, D. (2002) *Content Management Systems*, Birmingham, Glasshaus Publishing.
This book focuses on how to select a content management system. What marks it out is the clarity with which the somewhat complex issues of CM are presented, even though each chapter of the book is written by a different combination of authors. As well as highlighting the issues associated with selecting a commercial CMS the book also deals with open-source solutions and provides guidance (and some warnings) on building your own CMS. The authors go on to provide important advice on the issues of migration of legacy content, and on CM implementation.

Asprey, L. and Middleton, M. (2003) *Integrative Document and Content Management: strategies for exploiting enterprise knowledge*, Hershey, Idea Group Publishing.
The benefit of this very comprehensive handbook is that it goes beyond web content and addresses the selection and implementation of document management systems as well as web content management systems. The authors emphasize the importance of the initial work on understanding and documenting business processes and document life-cycles, and a valuable feature of the book is the level of detail on the function requirements of a document management system.

Boiko, B. (2002) *Content Management Bible*, New York, Hungry Minds.
This massive 966-page book was one of the first books to be
published on content management, and remains a definitive
textbook. It covers both the principles of content management
and how to implement a content management system, based on
the author's ten years of experience in this area. There is a
companion website at www.metatorial.com. Bob Boiko and Rita
Warren have also developed a CMS Metatorial Planner as a
companion to the book. This 168-page guide is designed to
provide a way for organizations to cope with the complexities of
the analysis and planning phases of the project. The Planner itself
is in a pdf format, but it comes with a number of Word
templates. These enable the team to work through the sections of
the Planner, and then paste the outcomes of the analysis work
into the templates for review and subsequent incorporation into a
request for proposal from vendors. A new edition of the *Content
Management Bible* is due to be published in late 2004.

Byrne, T., *The CMS Report*, CMS Watch, www.cmswatch.com.
This site is compiled with great skill by Tony Byrne, a leading
independent CMS consultant. The site provides access to news
stories, feature articles and reports. In late 2004 the first of a new
series of reports on other aspects of the enterprise content
management market was released, covering enterprise search
engines.

Laugero, G. and Globe, A. (2002) *Enterprise Content Services*, New
York, Addison-Wesley.
This book provides a mixture of advice on the strategic issues
involved in making a business case for a content management
system, and on how to carry out a content audit and manage the
implementation of a content management system. At 160 pages it
has far less detail than other titles listed here on the practical
aspects of CMS selection and implementation, but is quite a good
introduction to the subject.

Robertson, J. *Content Management Requirements Toolkit*, Step Two
Designs, Sydney, Australia, www.steptwo.com.au.
James Robertson has been involved in content management

projects for some time, and writes from practical experience. This *Toolkit* is designed to assist organizations prepare a statement of requirements for a content management system. Like the Metatorial Planner the 64-page *Toolkit* comes as a pdf file and also as a set of Word templates. The sections of the *Toolkit* deal with Content Creation, Content Management, Publishing, Presentation, and Contract and Business.

Rockley, A. with Kostur, P. and Manning, S. (2002) *Managing Enterprise Content: a unified content strategy*, Indianapolis, New Riders, www.newriders.com.
The focus of this 565-page book is, as the title indicates, the development and implementation of an enterprise content management strategy. There is a very good section on tools and technologies which sets out very clearly the questions that must be asked of any commercial content management software vendor. The human aspects of implementing a content management strategy are not overlooked either, with good chapters on implementation and managing change. The book concludes with appendices which provide a checklist for implementing a unified content strategy, writing for multiple media, content management vendors, a tools checklist and an introduction to content relationships.

Rosenfeld, L. and Morville, P. (2002) *Information Architecture for the World Wide Web*, 2nd edn, Sebastopol, CA, O'Reilly and Associates Inc.
Although not strictly about content management systems this book is essential reading on the subjects of information architecture, navigation design, search systems, thesauri and metadata. The book is illustrated with many examples of good practice and, as with all the other books in this section, is written by experts who have substantial practical experience in information architecture.

Useful websites

With so many web content management companies adapting their products and their business strategy towards enterprise content

management it is becoming increasingly difficult to track
developments in the market and the release of new products.

The following websites are just a personal selection of the many
hundreds of sites that provide information and advice on content
management, and between them provide links to just about every
web resource there is on content management topics.

Aifia
www.aifia.org

The Asilomar Institute for Information Architecture is a US-based
organization but it has an extensive international membership.
The site provides access to a range of resources that facilitate the
development of effective websites and intranets, and also runs an
excellent discussion forum for members.

Boxes and Arrows
www.boxesandarrows.com

This unusual website is not strictly about content management
systems but about information architecture and the design of
effective web and intranet sites. It is more like an electronic
journal because it is a collection of peer-reviewed papers but the
result is that the quality of the content is very high.

CMPros
www.cmprofessionals.org

CM Pros is a membership organization that fosters the sharing of
content management information practices and strategies. It was
set up in mid 2004 to represent the interests of anyone involved
in content management. The initial stimulus was from Bob Doyle,
the developer of CMS Review (see below). Membership of the
not-for-profit organization currently costs $50 per year. Although
based in Boston, USA, there is international representation on
the Board of Directors.

CMS Review
www.cmsreview.com

The mission of the site is to give the resources needed to choose
a content management system. Over the last year it has grown
into probably the most comprehensive resource there is on

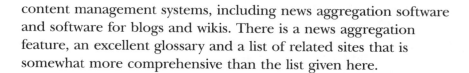

content management systems, including news aggregation software and software for blogs and wikis. There is a news aggregation feature, an excellent glossary and a list of related sites that is somewhat more comprehensive than the list given here.

Content Manager

www.contentmanager.net

This is without doubt the most comprehensive European-centric site and until early in 2004 was published only in German. A good English-language version of the site has recently been launched. The most valuable features of this site are the very comprehensive list of products and the fact that you can select and compare the features of selected packages in a standardized format.

Content Wire

www.content-wire.com

This site provides a news service on developments in content management, covering both technical and industry developments, and also issues related to content publishing. It is compiled by journalist Paola Di Maio and is updated daily Monday to Thursday. Paola is based in London and so the coverage of European developments is especially good.

CMS Watch

www.cmswatch.com

This site is compiled with great skill by Tony Byrne, a leading independent CMS consultant and the author of the CMS Watch report cited above. His site provides access to news stories, feature articles and reports, and also offers a good summary of the main CMS packages currently on the market. Tony also offers an e-mail newsletter service.

Findability

http://findability.org

This site is the work of Peter Morville, the co-author of *Information Architecture for the World Wide Web* (see p. 143). Findability is a concept that Peter has developed to encompass all aspects of content navigation and retrieval. The site provides a valuable set of links to core resources on this subject.

Gilbane Report
www.gilbane.com

The Gilbane Report is a widely read newsletter covering content management technologies; it was founded by Frank Gilbane in 1993. The site also contains good lists of other sites, and a wide range of white papers sponsored by industry vendors.

Hartman Communicatie
http://tools.hartman-communicatie.nl

This site is managed by Eric Hartmann and lists content management vendors in a matrix format that enables the CMS products from these vendors to be evaluated on a comparative basis. Some indication of price is also given. As a source of information on the smaller European CM vendors this site is invaluable.

Intranet Focus
www.intranetfocus.com

This website is maintained by Martin White. Although predominately about intranet management the site has a section on CMS topics, and a blog that also covers developments in CMS implementation and the CMS industry.

ProjectCMS
www.projectcms.com

This is a blog devoted to content management technology and implementation authored by Matthew Clapp and Brook Baldwin. The content is lively and opinionated, and the site also lists other blogs that cover content management developments.

StepTwo
www.steptwo.com.au

This site has been established by James Robertson, a leading Australian consultant on content management and knowledge management. James publishes excellent white papers on a wide range of CMS-related topics and the site provides a comprehensive list of CMS vendors. James also publishes a very useful blog at www.steptwo.com.au/columntwo/index.html.

Index